Sarah Payne is a popular quilting teacher, designer and TV demonstrator, well-known on *Create and Craft*. She started crafting at a young age, under her mother's watchful eye, but went on to study Economics and pursue a career in IT.

In 2011, Sarah decided to take a break and rediscover the creative side of her nature. She started by opening a fabric shop and training centre, before becoming a regular contributor to all the major UK quilting magazines. She has launched a successful range of quilting kits and now designs her own fabric range for Craft Cotton Company.

Sarah lives in Peterborough, UK. Her website is www.sarahpayne.co.uk.

SARAH PAYNE'S QUILT SCHOOL

Dedication

This book is dedicated to the memory of my darling dad, Julian Gray, who was always so proud of everything that I created.

SARAH PAYNE'S
QUILT SCHOOL

New ways to start patchwork and quilting

SARAH PAYNE

SEARCH PRESS

Acknowledgements

I would like to thank my mum,
Pauline Daniels, for inspiring me to pick up a
needle, my dad, Julian Gray for bringing me up
to realize I can be anything I want to be, and my
ever-patient partner Paul who often feels that
he plays second fiddle to my sewing machine
(which honestly, he doesn't).
Thank you to my friends and family for your
support and patience when I wasn't very
sociable because I was working on 'my
book'. Hopefully, normal service
will soon be resumed.

First published in 2019

Search Press Limited
Wellwood, North Farm Road,
Tunbridge Wells, Kent TN2 3DR

Text and templates copyright © Sarah Payne 2019

Photographs by Paul Bricknell at Search Press Studios
Photographs on pages 1–7, 26, 28, 33, 34, 35 (bottom right), 38, 39
(bottom), 42, 43 (top right), 46, 49, 52, 54 (bottom), 56, 58, 62, 64, 66
(bottom), 71 (background), 74, 75, 78, 81 (bottom right), 82 (top right), 85
(background), 86, 87, 89, 92–93 (background), 94, 95 (bottom), 99, 100
(top), 102, 103, 106 (bottom right), 108, 109 (right), 113, 121 (bottom), 122
(background), 127 (background) by Stacy Grant
Photograph on page 8 by Debbie Patterson

Photographs and design copyright © Search Press Ltd. 2019

ISBN: 978-1-78221-730-5

The Publishers and author can accept no responsibility for any
consequences arising from the information, advice or instructions
given in this publication.

Readers are permitted to reproduce any of the items in this book for
their personal use, or for the purposes of selling for charity, free of
charge and without the prior permission of the Publishers. Any use of
the items for commercial purposes is not permitted without the prior
permission of the Publishers.

Suppliers
If you have difficulty in obtaining any of the materials and equipment
mentioned in this book, then please visit the Search Press website for
details of suppliers: www.searchpress.com

You are invited to visit the author's website:
www.sarahpayne.co.uk

CONTENTS

INTRODUCTION

We all want to be able to produce lovely works of art, and
quilters are no exception. There is something so special about
a handmade, hand-crafted gift. So, I am here to show you how
to create beautiful patchwork and quilted projects simply,
quickly and easily. With the right tools and some top tips, you
will be producing fabulous sewn items in no time, either using
hand sewing or machine sewing, whichever you prefer. Perfect
patchwork requires precision and accurate cutting leads to
accurate sewing, and all of this leads to beautiful works of art.

I have been quilting for fifteen years. I know that doesn't
sound very long in the grand scheme of things, but it
certainly has been an interesting journey. As a child I learnt
to cross stitch, slowly and painfully producing a few very
wonky bookmarks, then I dabbled in dressing up my doll in
scraps left over from my mother's sewing table. At university
I turned to knitting toys for a little extra spending money, and
later a busy career in IT meant many a night away in hotels,
where I discovered the joys of beading. So, I have been crafting
since childhood, but a chance visit to a local fabric shop that
was running quilt classes was the moment that all changed. I
immediately bought a sewing machine, signed up to a year's
worth of sampler quilt classes, purchased a huge quantity of
fabric and set to it. I haven't stopped stitching since! It is no
exaggeration to say that I sew almost every day, and being
in my little sewing room surrounded with gorgeous fabric,
wondrous threads and fabulous colours gives me a great sense
of peace.

Now I want to share that love of quilting with you and show
you how you can create beautiful heirloom-quality quilted
items with the right tools.

Using this book

The instructions in this book build your
skills through the process of creating
stitched projects. I focus on different
shapes in turn: squares, triangles and
circles, with projects that you will love
to make.

Some sets of instructions allow you
to create projects of varying sizes, up
to a full quilt top. Guidance for layering,
quilting and binding techniques are at
the end of the book, unless they are an
integral part of the project. For each
project, I explain what quilting and
binding techniques I used, allowing
you to copy or experiment with your
own variations.

Many of these designs can be varied
to use different size blocks and pre-
cuts such as jelly rolls and charm packs.
Guidance is given on how to do this for
each project where appropriate.

A note on imperial and metric measurements

Quilt measurements are traditionally
noted in inches, and so all rulers are
marked in inches. However I also include
metric equivalents, rounded to the
nearest 10cm, for the yardage that you
need to purchase for each project.

When requirements are listed in the
book, it is assumed that measurements
are width of fabric unless otherwise
stated. This means that it will be based
on the whole width of fabric as it appears
on the bolt on the shelves in a shop. This
is usually 40–42in (101.5–106.5cm) wide.
If other measurements are required,
including precuts, they will be detailed
under each project.

Many of the requirements are
rounded up so you have room for
'mistakes'. Keep these extra pieces to
use for the scraps projects at the end of
the book.

TOOLS AND MATERIALS
CUTTING TOOLS

Accurate cutting is the secret to great patchwork. If you cut accurately, you have a neat fabric edge to follow and your seam allowance will be straight and accurate too.

There are a number of cutting machines on the market, but I use the 'old school' method – a rotary cutter, a mat and a ruler – you can see a picture of the ones I like to use below.

Rotary cutter There are several makes of rotary cutter available. Ensure that you invest in a good quality one, that fits comfortably in your hands. The moveable blades are super sharp, so you want to be safe. The most common size uses a 1¾in (45mm) blade and is perfect for most fabric cutting. If you are left-handed, make sure that you have one that is adaptable to your needs.

Rotary cutter blades are interchangeable between brands, as long as you have the correct size. Blades come in four sizes: ¾in (18mm), 1in (28mm), 1¾in (45mm) and 2in (60mm). The most useful size is 1¾in (45mm).

Replace the blades on your rotary cutter when they begin to get blunt, so that you always work with a sharp blade. A blunt blade can spoil the edge of the fabric and frustrate you. It can also make you 'wobble' as you apply extra pressure to get a decent cut. This can be uncomfortable, and dangerous. If you miss a spot at regular intervals, you have probably run over a pin at some point and ruined your blade. It will need replacing.

TIP

Rotary blades are sharp and should be treated carefully. If your cutter has a blade cover, always close it when not in use. Cut away from your body for obvious reasons!

Cutting mat Invest in a self-healing cutting mat. These have a special surface that closes after being cut with a sharp blade (hence the term 'self-healing').

There are a number of different sizes of mat available. Make sure that your mat is big enough for the fabric that you want to cut. Too small a mat will mean that you must fold your fabric a number of times and can lead to kinks in your straight lines. The largest of the portable quilting cutting mats is 24 x 36in (61 x 91.5cm). It's a nice size, but it's also quite large and not so portable. I leave this on my sewing table at home which is great for cutting large pieces of fabric. For your first mat, 18 x 24in (45.5 x 61cm) is the best size because you will comfortably be able to fit a fat quarter lengthwise on the mat without overhang and it is manageable for carrying to workshops.

Ensure your mat is clean and that there are not too many grooves cut in it where you plan to cut. Although they are self-healing, constantly cutting in the same place will create ridges and these affect accuracy.

Store your mat flat and keep away from heat – heat will make it bow out of shape which is really tricky to fix and will make decent cutting impossible.

Ruler Rulers are sometimes referred to as acrylics or templates, but they are basically all the same thing: thick plastic shapes that allow you to run your rotary cutter blade along the edge without slipping. Don't confuse them with stationery rulers or thin templates, neither of which are thick enough to give the blade the necessary support.

The best ruler to start with is a large 24 x 6 or 6½in (61 x 15 or 16.5cm) ruler like the EASY Rule II by Simplicity. This will enable you to trim fat quarters into smaller manageable pieces. Once you have had a play with these, you may consider getting different shape rulers. Square rulers are useful – my most commonly used sizes are 6½in (16.5cm) and 15in (38cm).

SEWING TOOLS

When choosing a sewing machine, you will need to know which feet will be most helpful for your quilting projects:

¼in (0.6cm) foot This foot will give you a consistent and accurate ¼in (0.6cm) seam allowance, which is important for ensuring precision.

Walking foot/dual feed foot/even feed foot This foot is known by many names, but it is essential for quilting together your layers. The dual feed ensures that all three layers of your quilt are pulled through the machine smoothly and it avoids unsightly puckering on the back of your finished project.

Free-motion/darning/embroidery foot This foot is used for free-motion quilting and certain types of free-motion embroidery. It is used when the feed dogs are lowered so you can move the fabric in all directions.

You may not need all these feet immediately, but they will soon become very important tools in your quilty kit.

Needles Getting the right needle can make the difference between an 'okay' job and a great job. Many issues with your sewing machine can be caused by incorrect or damaged needles. There are a couple of types of needle that are useful to have in your sewing box:

- Universal are the most commonly used needles to sew woven fabrics (such as those used for quilting) which have a warp and a weft, and a selvedge at the edges.
- Quilting needles are made especially for machine quilting. They have a special tapered and slightly rounded point which means the needle smoothly penetrates the fabric and helps eliminate skipped stitches. It has a stronger core to pierce through multiple layers of fabric and wadding.

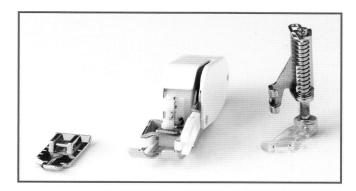

From left to right: ¼in (0.6cm) foot, walking foot, free-motion foot.

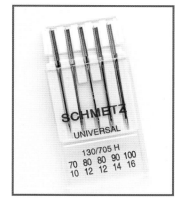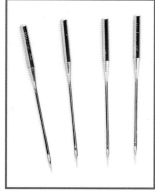

Sewing machine needles come in a variety of sizes. European sizes range from 60 to 120 and American sizes from 9 to 20. Most needles are marked with both sizes, and the lower the number, the finer the needle. Some packs of needles come with more than one size, but I usually use 80/12 for lightweight fabrics and 90/14 for medium weight fabrics such as quilting cottons and linen.

OTHER TOOLS IN MY SEWING BOX

1 Pins Some teachers tell you to pin everything, and others will raise their hands in horror if you undertake the time-consuming tasking of pinning every seam. Personally, I pin when necessary and no more often than that. My personal favourites are flower-headed pins because you can stitch straight up to them on the sewing machine without any distortion. However, glass-headed pins are useful because they won't melt when you need to iron the fabric with pins in place, and tiny appliqué pins are perfect for securing little appliquéd shapes in place. You will of course find your own favourites, but rest assured, you will never have enough pins!

2 Quilter's masking tape This is incredibly useful for marking out quilting lines. It is exactly ¼in (0.6cm) wide and so is also great for checking seams. Unlike traditional masking tape, it is low tack and therefore will not pull the fibres in your fabric when you remove it from your project. Despite this, never leave it on your fabric longer than you need to in case it leaves a mark.

3 Needles You can never have too many sewing needles. Sharps size 9 or 10 are good for piecing or appliqué, and Betweens 9 or 10s are great for quilting. Even if you are not quilting by hand, you may want to bury the loose ends of your quilting threads once you have completed your machine quilting – and you will require a needle for that. In this instance, choose one with a sharp tip and a longer eye because it saves time to thread both thread ends in one go.

4 Fabric markers There are a wide range of fabric markers available, including chalk wheels and air-, water- or heat-erasable pens. They are all good for their particular jobs and are available in a wide range of colours to show up on your projects. However, markers should be used with care, and checked on all the fabrics that you intend to use to be sure that they will completely disappear. It would be a shame to mark out your quilting lines only for the ink to be permanent. Be aware that ironing many of these pens can actually heat set the ink, so ensure that you have removed the ink before pressing.

5 Seam ripper (reverse stitcher) This is the most used item in my sewing box! It is useful for fixing those tricky mistakes, but you really shouldn't get too obsessed with it. It is easy to get so consumed by the need for perfection that you spend more time undoing than doing. As a rule, if I think I will notice the mistake when I look at in a month's time, then it is worth taking the time to remove it. Otherwise, I take a deep breath and keep stitching.

The blade of your seam ripper will blunt over time, so when it doesn't remove those stitches as well as it used to, throw it away and get a new one. Pulling the stitches with a blunt blade can distort or damage your fabric, as well as frustrate you.

6 Scissors No sewing box is complete without scissors. Using a rotary cutter is quicker, but you will still need to cut fabrics, paper and thread. Get a good pair of medium-sized scissors for fabric and another pair for cutting paper – but do not mix the two (I tie a ribbon around the handle of my fabric scissors so I don't confuse them). Cutting paper or card will ruin your lovely fabric scissors in no time. Small, sharp scissors are perfect for cutting loose threads and cutting into curved seams.

7 Microstitch This tool is easy to use and saves time on basting your quilt layers. Using small tacks, the small, extra fine needle shoots the tiny micro fasteners through the fabrics which can be sewn over and easily removed with a quick snip.

8 Spray glue Temporary spray adhesives are used to stick your layers of fabric together. These colourless specialist fabric glues are designed not to gum up your needle as you sew, and will wash out once you have finished your project.

9 Wonder clips These are great for keeping bulky projects (i.e. wadded ones) together.

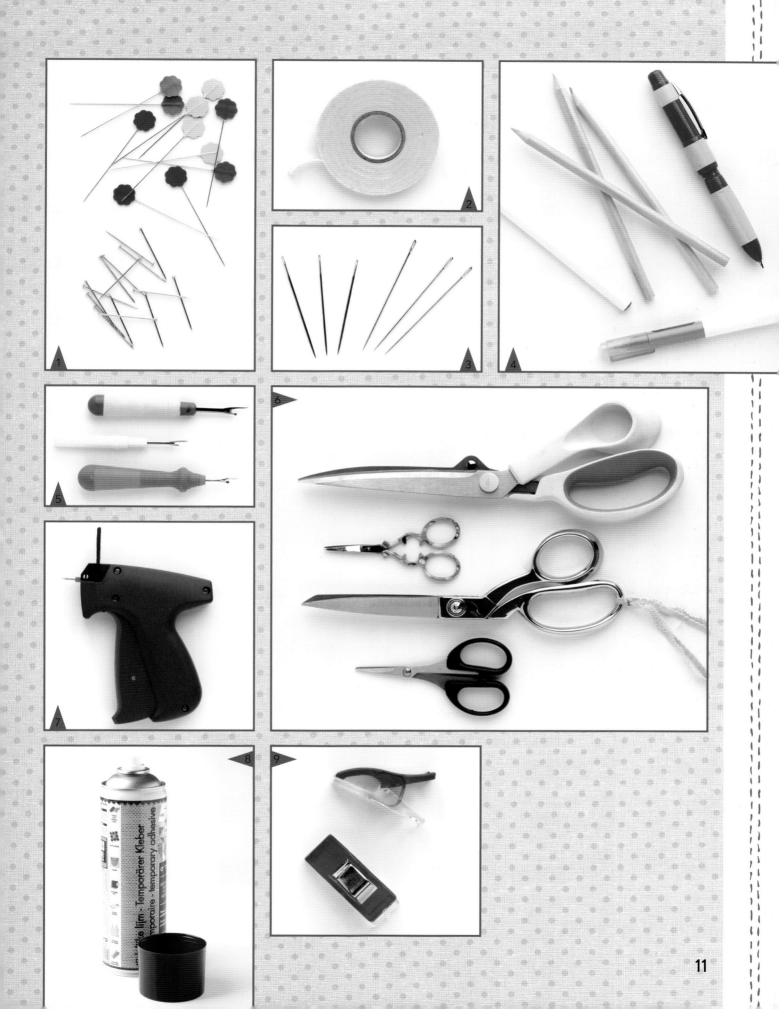

FABRICS

We have looked at the tools you will need for your quilting projects; now you need to think about the materials. The easiest fabrics to begin with are medium weight 100% cotton, often labelled as quilting weight cotton. These cut easily and wash well and will play nicely with other 100% medium weight cottons. Light weaves can stretch, and tightly woven fabrics can be hard to quilt. Stick to medium weights and your journey will start off far more smoothly.

Once you have chosen your fabric, it is important to understand how it behaves, and when to use these behaviours to your advantage!

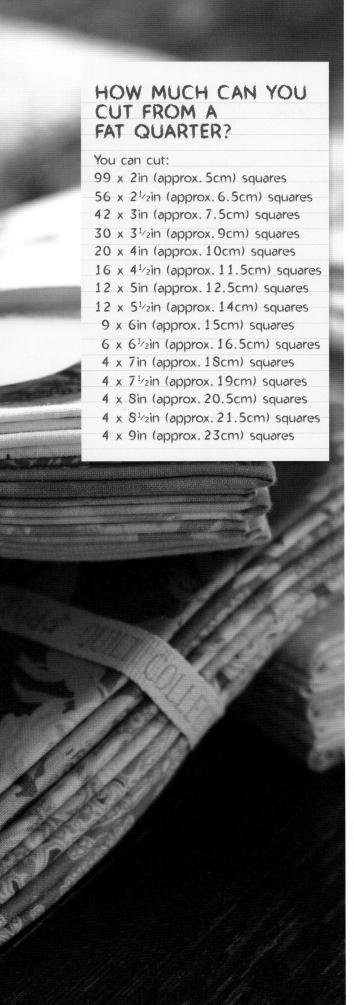

HOW MUCH CAN YOU CUT FROM A FAT QUARTER?

You can cut:

99 x 2in (approx. 5cm) squares
56 x 2½in (approx. 6.5cm) squares
42 x 3in (approx. 7.5cm) squares
30 x 3½in (approx. 9cm) squares
20 x 4in (approx. 10cm) squares
16 x 4½in (approx. 11.5cm) squares
12 x 5in (approx. 12.5cm) squares
12 x 5½in (approx. 14cm) squares
9 x 6in (approx. 15cm) squares
6 x 6½in (approx. 16.5cm) squares
4 x 7in (approx. 18cm) squares
4 x 7½in (approx. 19cm) squares
4 x 8in (approx. 20.5cm) squares
4 x 8½in (approx. 21.5cm) squares
4 x 9in (approx. 23cm) squares

Pre-cuts

Fabric pre-cuts are a fun and easy way to get started, because the cutting has been done for you and you can get straight on with the sewing. You can also be sure that the fabrics selected will always look right in your project because the fabrics are designed to go together.

Many of the projects in this book can be created using pre-cuts, and advice will be given for adapting the patterns.

Fat quarters

If you know anything about sewing you will have heard of a fat quarter. They are one of the most commonly purchased fabric sizes because they allow beginners to get a number of fabrics that work together without too much outlay.

Fat quarters are often sold in co-ordinating bundles and come in very useful sizes, e.g. five, six or ten fat quarters. If you want to, you can go into your local shop and treat yourself to a fat quarter from the whole range!

A fat quarter is a cut of fabric that (usually) measures 19.5 x 22in (50 x 56cm) (if based on a metre) or 18 x 22in (45.5 x 56cm) (if based on a yard).

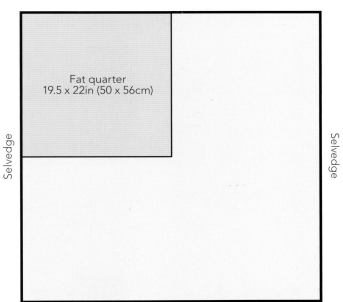

Fat quarter
19.5 x 22in (50 x 56cm)

Selvedge

Selvedge

TIP

This book is based on UK fat quarters. If you have purchased your fabric from the US, bear in mind that the fat quarter may be slightly smaller, so check before you begin cutting.

Jelly rolls (or fabric rolls)

These are 2½in (6.5cm) wide strips cut from selvedge to selvedge. They are a family of fabrics that all work together and can be used to great effect in scrappy quilts. The number of strips in a jelly roll can vary by manufacturer, so do check you have enough strips for your project. There are also 1½in (4cm) wide strips called honey buns, although these are a lot less common.

Charm packs

These are 5in (12.5cm) square pieces of fabric just ready and waiting to be stitched together – no fuss. The number of squares in a pack can vary depending on the manufacturer, and there will often be duplicates from the range.

Layer cakes

These are the big daddy of the charm packs because they are 10in (25.5cm) squares. Again, they are pre-cut, so you can get stitching, but these can also be cut into four pieces to make 5in (12.5cm) squares, used to make large half square triangles (HSTs) or even quarter square triangles (QSTs).

Jelly rolls.

Layer cakes.

Charm packs.

Choosing colours

Choosing the colours of your fabrics can be one of the most daunting challenges as a sewer – both for beginners and the more experienced. Here are some ideas to help you get over this first hurdle.

Families of fabric

Fabric designers create their collections in 'families' and they often produce twenty or thirty different fabrics that are intended to work together. There will be colours that complement each other, and elements that are repeated throughout the range. Manufacturers then package some of these fabrics into fat quarter bundles making it easy for you to collect fabrics for your next project.

You could also choose a 'theme' for your project and build the design that way. For example, a popular baby quilt project is an 'I spy' quilt. 'I spy' quilts are created with pictorial or novelty fabrics printed with objects that might not be obvious from a distance but can be identified during a closer look at the quilt. These are often made for young children who are encouraged to search through and identify small objects in the fabrics with the game 'I spy with my little eye'. For this kind of pattern, the fabrics are busy, bright and full of small objects. Putting together fabrics that you would never think of is integral to this design.

Value

Value is a term we talk about a lot in patchwork. It means the relative lightness or darkness of one fabric over another. A fabric may be medium in one fabric group, and dark relative to another group of fabrics. In patchwork, the value can be very important, and we often choose a range of light, medium and dark values to add interest to a design.

Choosing a contrasting colour

You may find that you have a great selection of fabrics for your project, but then you need to find a contrasting colour to pull the design together. I am a great fan of using a white design on a white background (called a tone on tone print) in my quilts. I find that this looks so much better than using a plain white fabric as it adds depth to a design. Black also works well as a contrast, as it can brighten the palette once it is added to your design. Neutrals like grey or ecru can also work well. Once you have chosen your main fabrics, you can always 'audition' your contrast by laying your chosen fabrics alongside a piece of the contrasting fabric. You will be surprised by how different a range of fabrics can look when you change the contrast.

These families of fabrics have been chosen to work together and complement each other.

Selvedge

The selvedge is the finished edge of the fabric as it comes off the bolt. It keeps the fabric from unravelling or fraying and can have important information about the fabric printed on it – like the name of the fabric, the designer and the colours used in creating the design. This information can be useful when buying more fabric if you run out.

We don't include a selvedge in standard patchwork because it often uses a different weave to the main fabric. You should avoid using it in projects as it can be glaringly obvious if included accidentally. The extra thickness can create lumps and bumps, and there are sometimes tiny holes in the selvedge, made when the fabric runs through the dying machines, that can spoil the look of your work. However, there are many projects that make use of its decorative features.

Many quilt patterns will tell you to cut your strips from selvedge to selvedge so it can be a good idea to take note of where the selvedge is.

Fabric grain

There are three directions of cut that we use as quilters, and each has their uses:
- Bias cut
- Cross grain
- Straight grain

Bias cut Cut diagonally to the direction of the weave in the fabric, this is very stretchy. Pieces cut out on the bias must be treated carefully as they can stretch. Starching your fabric before cutting can help with this. We will talk more about bias stretch in the section on triangles. We can also make use of this stretch when cutting circles or creating binding that we want to stitch around curves.
How is it used?
- Bias cuts are most commonly used for binding quilts with curved edges so that the binding lays flat as it curves around the outer edges.
- Bias strips are often used to cover piping as it easily curves around the edges of a project and gives a very professional finish.
- Strips can also be used in appliqué designs because they can be curved. Bias cut edges also turn under more easily when working with appliqué shapes.

Cross grain This has less stretch than the bias cut, but more than the straight grain. It runs perpendicular to the selvedge (so you are cutting selvedge to selvedge).
How is it used?
- Most quilt patterns instruct you to cut cross grain strips and then cut them into patches.
- If the quilt will not be hung, quilt backs can be made with the cross grain running from side to side to economize on fabric.
- Cross grain binding is used for binding quilts with straight outside edges.

Straight grain Also called lengthwise grain, this has the least amount of stretch and it runs parallel to the selvedge of your fabric.
How is it used?
- You can reduce sagging in your quilts by cutting your fabric in ways that take advantage of the stability of straight grain. This is useful if the quilt will be hung on a wall.

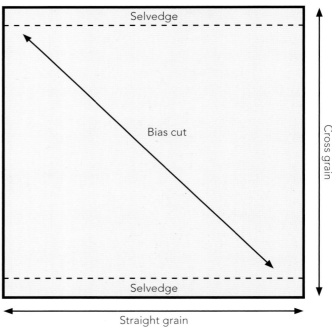

THREADS

The choice of threads is an important one. Always go for the best quality you can afford. Old or cheap thread may break, and can limit the life of your project. I personally feel that it would be a shame to spend money on fabrics and time on construction, only to waste it all by cutting corners on the thread.

For piecing, you want a good, strong, neutral-coloured thread. Start collecting colours from ecru (for piecing with light fabrics) all the way through to dark grey (for dark colours), but avoid piecing with white or black because these can be too stark a contrast and can even show through your fabrics. Do not waste your more glamorous (or more expensive) threads on piecing because they will not be seen once your project is completed. Save these for topstitching or quilting where they can be enjoyed.

In this book I have used Gütermann and WonderFil threads for eye-catching finishes and detailed stitching.

Here you can see the range of colourful threads I use.

WADDING/BATTING

Another material you need to consider is wadding. This is the soft layer of material used between the backing and quilt top. It is known as batting in the US. There are a number of different varieties of wadding/batting and they can be used to achieve different results. You will learn which ones are your favourite as you get more experienced.

'Loft' refers to the depth or 'poofiness' of your wadding/batting and is a term you may come across when investigating which wadding to use. A low loft means the wadding is quite thin, whereas a high loft means it is thick.

Choose a low loft wadding if you want your finished project to have a flatter appearance and for a fluffier quilt, choose a high loft wadding.

How is wadding made?

Needle punched wadding This is where fibres are needle punched or dry felted together to create uniform layers that are strongly fused and create a soft drape. The more the fibres are punched together, the denser the resulting wadding. Needle punched wadding requires very close quilting – often stitching no further than about 4in (10cm) apart. The needle punched fibres are easy to glide a needle through, so are perfect for the hand-quilting enthusiast.

Needle punched wadding with scrim Scrim is a lightweight sheet of stabilizer that is needle punched into the wadding as it is formed to add strength, durability, and to support the finished item when it is washed. This stability also enables you to quilt much further apart, allowing stitching lines 8–10in (20.5–25.5cm) apart.

Thermal bonded wadding Thermal bonding is used for fibres like polyester or wool. Needle punching for these fibres could cause fibre migration (or bearding) where the finished wadding has a 'fuzz' and would easily show through the resulting quilt. To avoid this, a small amount of 'low melt' polyester is mixed in with the wadding fibres and then passed through a warm oven to melt them together. Thermally bonded polyester has a higher loft (height) and is very lightweight and 'poofy'! This can add real dimension and definition to the quilting. Thermal bonding in high loft wadding often requires a stitched area of 4in (10cm). But do not worry, the packaging on your wadding will usually tell you how close you need to quilt.

Should I pre-shrink?

Some wadding will shrink depending on the fibre content – and this is usually noted on the packaging so make sure you keep a note once you have removed it. 100% cotton and wool blends tend to shrink the most. This can be used to create the 'antique' look that many quilters desire by washing after the quilt has been completed. If you do not want to achieve this effect, you should pre-shrink. To pre-shrink your wadding, submerge in warm water (not hot) and soak for twenty minutes. Gently squeeze out excess water by rolling it in a dry towel. Be careful as wet wadding is very fragile. To dry your wadding, lay it flat or put in a warm dryer for a short time.

Different types of wadding

We know that there are different types of wadding available, so how do you decide which ones to use?

Polyester This wadding has many advantages for the quilter. It is lightweight and durable – it will spring back into shape no matter how many times it is washed. It is washable by hand or by machine, so it is easy to care for and is perfect for items that require frequent washing such as play mats. It is good for those with allergies because there are no allergens in it. Polyester is the least expensive option and available in a wide range of lofts or thicknesses. Wadding with a higher loft is great for showing quilt stitch definition and it is ideal for bags and items of haberdashery that are frequently used because of its durability.

100% cotton Cotton is a firm favourite with quilters who like the antique/heirloom look and the pleasure of working with pure cotton. It has been used since the earliest days of quilting and is still hugely popular today. It is soft and can be quilted with a lot of detail. Cotton is washable by hand or machine (on a cool wash). It is great for hand quilting because a needle passes through the fibres easily. Cotton won't melt if you put a hot pan on it, so it is perfect for table runners, placemats etc. 100% cotton is ideal for giving your quilt that heirloom look, as it shrinks (about 3–5%) and wrinkles the first time you wash it. It also works well for summer quilts as it is light and breathable.

Cotton/polyester blend The best of both worlds and my wadding of choice! It has the light low loft feel and breathability of cotton with the durability and safe washing of polyester. Popular blends are 80% cotton/ 20% polyester and 60% cotton/40% polyester. A blended material is a good choice for quilters who are unsure which wadding is the best for their quilts. Cotton and polyester blended wadding is typically less expensive than pure cotton but pricier than completely polyester products. It can be used to make pretty much anything you like.

Wool is the warmest of the waddings on the market and is the best choice for quilts which are used in damp and cool climates as they are able to absorb moisture. It is too warm for spring and summer use but is popular with both hand and machine quilters. Wool is lightweight and retains its loft throughout the life of the quilt, making it popular with art quilters. Wool is not as easy to keep as the other options because it can attract moths if not stored correctly and it can be tricky to wash – and should never be tumble dried! It is also a pricey option.

There are other waddings available on the market, including bamboo and silk. Eventually, the choice of wadding is personal. It can be based on how you plan to use the finished quilt, how you want to quilt it, what look you want it to have or how much money you can afford to spend.

Wadding – the flat wadding has a low loft and the puffier wadding has a high loft.

BASIC TECHNIQUES

CUTTING ACCURATELY

Perfect patchwork requires precision – and the best place to start is with accurate cutting. If you can cut a nice straight line, then you have a guide to follow with your stitching. If your pieces are cut true, they will be easier to match up when you come to stitch them together, making the whole process easier and more fun. Here are some tips on getting a decent cut with your rotary cutter, ruler and cutting mat.

Location

Find somewhere comfortable to cut. Bending too much can cause back pain and will affect your accuracy as well as your enjoyment of cutting.

Make sure that your surface is flat. Bumps underneath the mat will prevent even pressure being applied to your cutting.

Good lighting is always important – you need to be able to see the markings on your ruler.

Tools

You will need: a cutting mat, a rotary cutter and blades, and a ruler. Always use the right ruler for the job. Trying to cut small squares with a large square can be clumsy and cutting a large square with a small ruler is tricky to do accurately.

Rotary cutters and a cutting mat.

Practice!

You will only learn how much pressure to apply when cutting by practising! You shouldn't need to work up a sweat – if you do, then you may need a new blade…

TIP

If you sit down when you are cutting, it is easy to apply forward pressure which can accidentally shift the ruler. It is therefore better to stand up when you are cutting.

1   Make sure you have the correct placement of hands when cutting. Spread your fingers across the ruler to stop it moving, but ensure your index finger is away from the edge of the ruler for safety.

2   When you hold your ruler, try to push downwards rather than forwards, because forward pressure can cause the ruler to shift as you cut. Always cut away from your body, in case you slip.

3   When you cut fabric, you can hear the blade cutting through the layers – it makes a 'woosh' sound. If you can't hear it, you are probably not cutting!

4   Do not move your ruler until you are sure that you have cut the fabric all the way, because it can be hard to line it up with your fabric again later.

An accurately cut piece of fabric.

SEWING ACCURATELY

As we discussed in the previous section, the secret to good sewing is starting with good cutting. Now we know how to do that well using the correct tools, let's move onto the sewing part.

Whether you hand or machine sew is personal choice. Many people like the slow pace of hand sewing, as the rhythmic movement of needle through cloth can be relaxing. However, this is a much slower method for creating quilts, so if speed is required, then a machine is the best way to go.

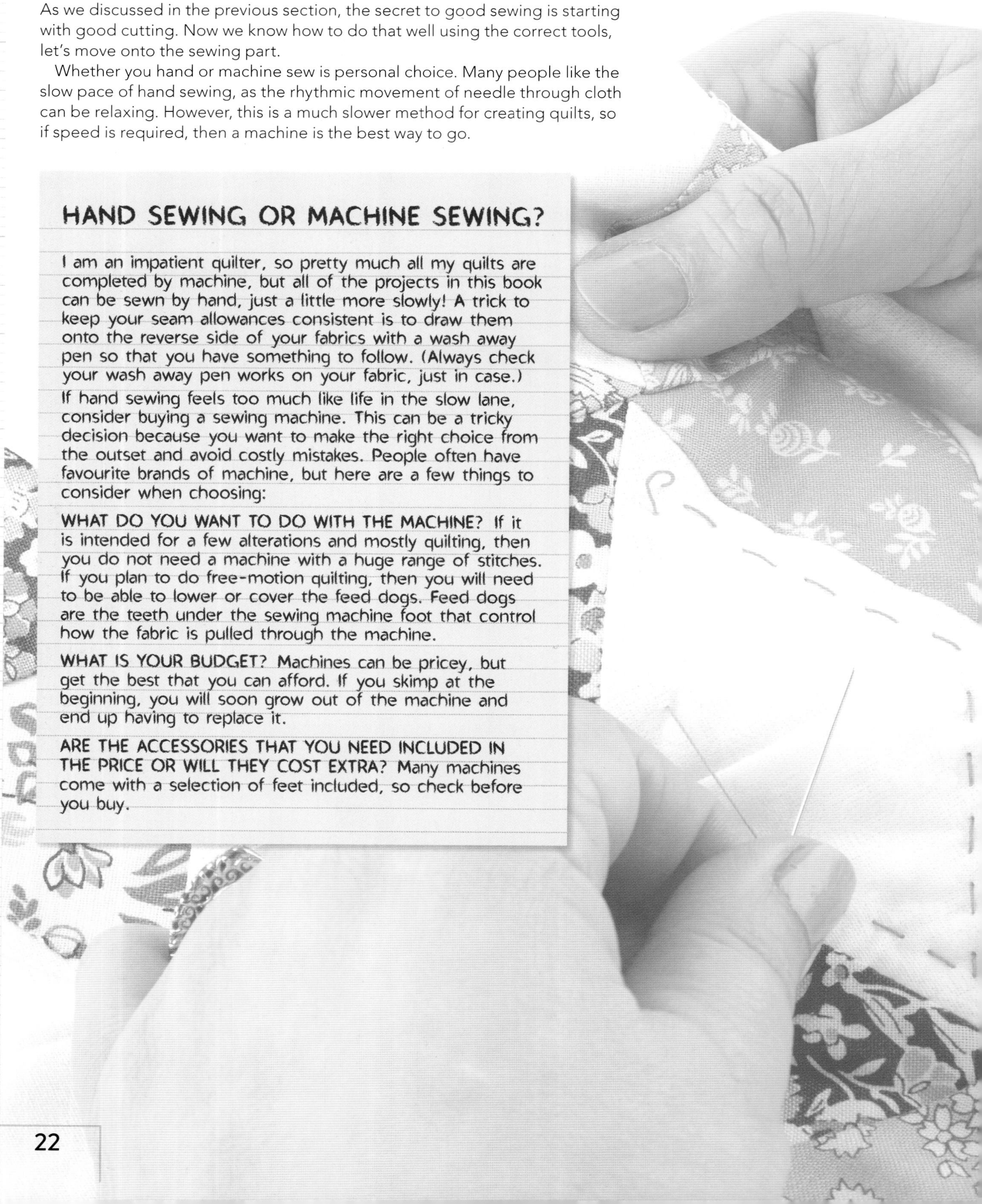

HAND SEWING OR MACHINE SEWING?

I am an impatient quilter, so pretty much all my quilts are completed by machine, but all of the projects in this book can be sewn by hand, just a little more slowly! A trick to keep your seam allowances consistent is to draw them onto the reverse side of your fabrics with a wash away pen so that you have something to follow. (Always check your wash away pen works on your fabric, just in case.)

If hand sewing feels too much like life in the slow lane, consider buying a sewing machine. This can be a tricky decision because you want to make the right choice from the outset and avoid costly mistakes. People often have favourite brands of machine, but here are a few things to consider when choosing:

WHAT DO YOU WANT TO DO WITH THE MACHINE? If it is intended for a few alterations and mostly quilting, then you do not need a machine with a huge range of stitches. If you plan to do free-motion quilting, then you will need to be able to lower or cover the feed dogs. Feed dogs are the teeth under the sewing machine foot that control how the fabric is pulled through the machine.

WHAT IS YOUR BUDGET? Machines can be pricey, but get the best that you can afford. If you skimp at the beginning, you will soon grow out of the machine and end up having to replace it.

ARE THE ACCESSORIES THAT YOU NEED INCLUDED IN THE PRICE OR WILL THEY COST EXTRA? Many machines come with a selection of feet included, so check before you buy.

Hand sewing

Hand sewing is becoming more and more popular as people see the joy in slowing down. A hand-sewn project is also more portable (because you don't have to lug a big, heavy machine around). I have used a dark thread so you can see my stitches, but you would use a neutral thread.

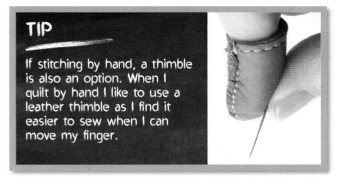

TIP

If stitching by hand, a thimble is also an option. When I quilt by hand I like to use a leather thimble as I find it easier to sew when I can move my finger.

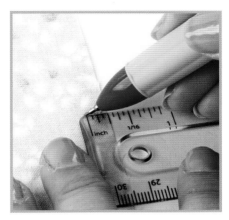

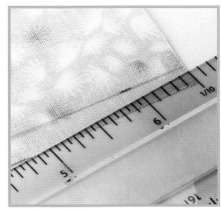

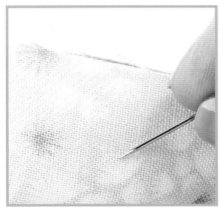

1   First, use a pen to mark the seam allowance onto the wrong side of the fabric to give yourself a line to follow.

2   Pin your two pieces of fabric together.

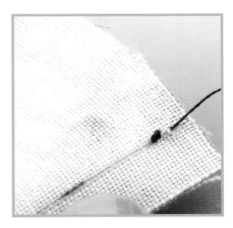

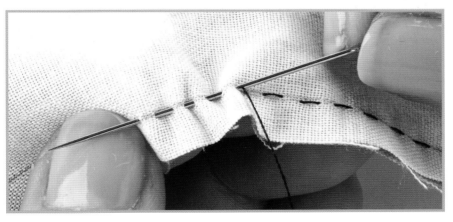

3   Begin and end each stitching line with a small knot or a back stitch to secure your stitching. Hand-stitched seams are more likely to come apart if they are not secured properly.

4   The stitch most commonly used for hand piecing is the running stitch. Simply pass the needle in and out of the fabric, making the topstitches equal in length. The stitches on the underside of the fabric may be shorter than the topside, but still even in length.

Machine sewing

When using a sewing machine it is not necessary to mark a stitch line. Place your fabric pieces right sides together and pin. Guide the raw edges of the fabric along the edge of the presser foot on the machine. Here I am using a ¼in (0.6cm) foot. Many machines have a ¼in (0.6cm) stitch, or a ¼in (0.6cm) foot. Many machines will allow you to move the needle position until you get a ¼in (0.6cm) seam allowance. If your machine will not allow you to move the needle position, you can mark the plate of your machine with a bit of masking tape to keep it accurate. It is important to get the seam allowance correct, because an overgenerous seam allowance can mean the difference between blocks fitting together, and not!

Always check your first few seams for accuracy. Be careful when returning to your machine after a break. Ensure that you set it up correctly again, especially if you have switched it off, because any changes to the machine will return to the default. It can help to make a note of the needle position on a scrap of paper and pin it to one of your blocks. This will prevent the need to work it all out again.

If you find that your sewing machine stitches are not even and smooth, you may have a problem with your tension. The tension dial is the mechanism that keeps the thread passing evenly through your fabric and stopping any puckering. Your manual is usually very useful for sorting out a tension issue, but the basics are as follows:

- If the bottom thread is showing on the top of the fabric then the top tension is too tight. Loosen by turning the tension dial to a lower number.
- If the top thread is being pulled onto the back of the fabric, then the top tension is too loose. Tighten it by turning the tension dial to a higher number.

Your tension may need to be changed when you work with different fabrics or threads. If you need to change the tension for a particular project, then it is a good idea to write the settings down on a piece of paper and pin it to your project for future reference.

Here I am guiding the raw edges of the fabric along the edge of the presser foot.

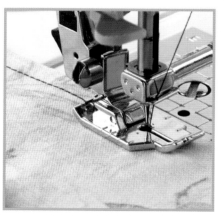

Here you can see the straight stitch in dark thread.

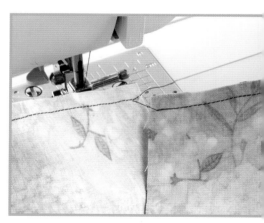

Chain piecing

Here are two pairs I have chain pieced. Chain piecing is the technique of sewing a number of blocks in an assembly line. To chain piece, feed your blocks through the machine one after another without stopping and without breaking the threads. Once completed, cut between the blocks.

PRESSING

There is a big difference between ironing and pressing: **Ironing** is what you do to your shirts! The iron slides across the fabric to remove all those pesky wrinkles, often with a lot of steam. This is not what we want to do to our quilts!

Pressing is what we do when we are piecing our quilts. For best results, you should press every seam once you have stitched it. Pressing involves placing your iron onto the seam, and then lifting it off before reapplying somewhere else.

To steam or not to steam?

Steam can cause more arguments among quilters than you would expect! Many say never steam because it can distort the fabrics, and once the fabric is washed and returns to its 'undistorted' state it may result in unsightly wrinkles. However, careful steam pressing can help you square-up a wonky block, and steam pressing produces crisply pressed seam allowances and fabrics. Personally, I like to keep a spray bottle of water next to my ironing board for when I need that little extra bit of oomph and avoid using steam. Stubborn creases may require a spritz!

Pressing seam allowances open

There are times when it is preferable to press the seams flat (or open) such as when lots of seams come together in one spot, creating too much bulk. Hand quilting can be easier when the seam allowances are flatter because it is easier to pass the needle through when there are fewer layers of fabric.

Pressing to 'The Dark Side'

This is a phrase often uttered by quilters and you may wonder what it means. If you are trying to match up seams in a block, it is good to press the seams to one side. We choose the darker of the two fabrics (the dark side) because the seam is less likely to show through the darker of the fabrics.

What happens when there is not a dark side? In this case, press to the more patterned fabric so the seam is less likely to show. Like most things in quilting, this is not a hard and fast rule: you may be asked to press 'in opposite directions' when pressing to the dark side won't work. Usually, a pattern will specify which direction you should press the seams.

Pressing the seam

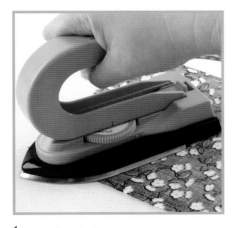

1 Lay the block on your ironing surface, just as it was sewn. Put the iron on top of the block to 'set the seam'.

2 Make sure that the fabric you want the seam to be pressed towards is on the top and flip back the fabric. Place the edge of the iron on the piece of fabric and gently work it towards and over the seam allowance. Use the weight of the iron to flatten the seam and try to avoid stretching the fabric.

3 Turn the block over and press from the back. Always press from the front before pressing from the back, or you may inadvertently press a tuck into the seam allowance. This would be a shame after taking all that effort to be accurate with the cutting, and then the sewing, just to spoil it now.

Here is the back of the finished seam, pressed to perfection!

SQUARES

Squares are the most basic shape in quilting, and the easiest place to start.
Each side of the square is the same size, and all the sides will be on the
straight grain so it doesn't stretch as much as other shapes.
The following section covers several projects using squares, and you can
adapt the designs by changing the size of your squares.

CUTTING SQUARES

There is a basic formula that will help you when cutting your squares. You simply need to add ¼in (0.6cm) around each of the four sides for the seam allowance.

So if you want a 6in (15cm) finished square (once it is sewn into a block) you simply need to add ½in (1.5cm) to your cut block (¼in (0.6cm) for either side).

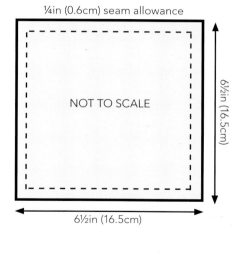

¼in (0.6cm) seam allowance

NOT TO SCALE

6½in (16.5cm)

6½in (16.5cm)

Cutting squares with a rotary cutter

This is one of the easiest methods of cutting multiple squares. To quickly and accurately cut squares, cut strips across the width of your fabric and then cut into squares. Using a rotary cutter and ruler allows you to cut multiple layers at the same time, making the whole process much quicker. If your rotary cutter starts to catch in the fabric, it is time to replace the blade.

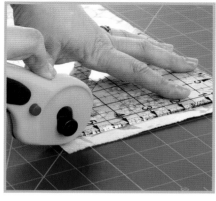

1 Start by cutting off the raw edge.

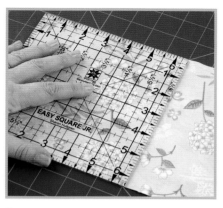

2 Now, turn your fabric around.

3 Cut your first square and keep cutting until you have all the squares you need.

Cutting squares with scissors

This method is slower and less accurate, but it does mean that you don't need to wait until you have all the equipment to get started. It is also useful if you are hand stitching because you don't need to rely on a straight edge to gauge your seam allowance.

With this method you should only cut one layer of fabric at a time, as it will have a tendency to shift when you pick it up to cut with scissors.

1 Make a template by using a ruler and a pencil to accurately draw your square onto paper, then cut it out.

2 Pin the template to your fabric.

3 Use scissors to cut around the template. Hold the fabric flat as you cut, otherwise it will move.

SIMPLY SQUARES SHOPPING BAG

Now we have got all our tools ready, it is time to start making.

This is a nice project to start with. Not only is it simple to create and possible to make in a day, it is a very useful bag to take with you next time you go fabric shopping. You can use a charm pack or simply cut your own 5in (12.5cm) squares. For this project I have used a layer cake pre-cut bundle called 'Freya and Friends' by Janet Clare, produced by Moda.

The finished bag is 18in (45.5cm) square.

You will need:

- Eight fat eighths or forty-eight charm pack pieces (5in (12.5cm) squares), or twelve pieces of a layer cake (10in (25.5cm) squares)
- 19¾in (50cm) of lining fabric
- 23½in (60cm) of wadding (optional)

Cutting instructions

Make sure you iron all the fabric before you cut for accuracy.

Cut six 5in (12.5cm) squares from each of the eight different fabrics. You need thirty-two for the bag and sixteen for the handles (forty-eight in total). If you are using the layer cake pieces, then cut each of your 10in (25.5cm) pieces into four 5in (12.5cm) squares.

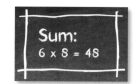

Sum:
6 x 8 = 48

Sewing instructions

1 Arrange sixteen squares in a loose chequerboard pattern of four rows of four squares, alternating between light and dark fabrics.

2 Sew the blocks together a row at a time. Take the first two squares and lay them right sides together (printed sides) and sew using a ¼in (0.6cm) seam along one edge. Then add the next square and sew to the last one.

3 Continue until you have finished the whole row. Press the seams towards the darker fabric.

4 Sew the next row in the same way but press the seams in the opposite direction to the first row. If you are alternating between light and dark squares then they will naturally be pressed in opposite directions.

5 Continue until all four rows are sewn and pressed.

6 Now take the first and second rows and place them right sides together, matching up the squares. Because you have pressed the seams in opposite directions they should snuggle into each other, making them easier to match up.

7 It can be useful to pin each intersecting point and both ends of the row. After sewing together, open up the rows and press in one direction.

8 Continue in the same way until all your rows are sewn together and pressed. Repeat for the other side of the bag.

The next stage is optional – wadding is not necessary, and if you do not want to include it in your bag then skip on to the next stage of construction.

Adding wadding as a variation

Wadding will give the bag a nice structure. If you want your bag to fold up into a small bundle for shopping, then leave out this wadding stage.

TIP

When approaching a corner, leave your needle down and pivot the fabric for a nice corner.

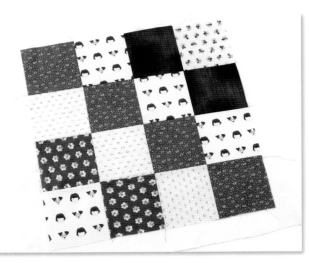

1   Cut your wadding about 2in (5cm) wider all the way around than your bag piece. This allows for any movement while quilting. Baste the patchwork bag front onto the wadding. You can use any of the layering methods covered on page 110 to attach the two layers (you do not need a backing for this project).

2   Quilt as desired, using any of the quilting methods covered on pages 111–119. For my example, I chose to use my walking foot to echo quilt ¼in (0.6cm) either side of the seams in a matching thread. This is a relatively small patchwork project, so can be used as a practice piece for developing your quilting skills. Trim the quilted patchwork bag pieces to size and continue constructing your bag.

Here is a variation using different fabric. This one is not quilted.

Constructing the outside of the bag

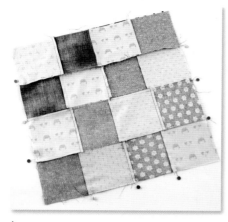

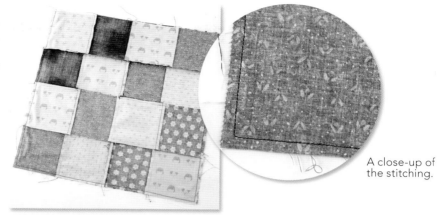

A close-up of the stitching.

1 Carefully pin the front and the back pieces together, lining up the ends of the rows so that they match. This example has no wadding.

2 With a ¼in (0.6cm) seam allowance, stitch around the edge of the bag in a 'U' shape, leaving the opening at the top. Use a back stitch at either end of your stitching to avoid the pieces coming apart. If you have wadded your bag, then a walking foot will be useful at this point. Trim any loose threads otherwise they can get caught behind the paler fabric and show through.

Making the lining

Making the handles

Cut two pieces of lining fabric, each measuring 18½in (47cm) square. Pin the squares right sides together and sew around three sides of the lining in a 'U' shape, leaving a 6in (15cm) gap in the bottom for turning through. It is a good idea to do a back stitch at either side of the gap so that the pieces don't come apart later.

1 Stitch the remaining sixteen squares into two rows of eight blocks to create two handle pieces measuring approximately 37in (94cm) each. Press the seams open to reduce bulk. If the straps are too long for you, trim to a suitable length.

2 Fold one of the handle pieces in half lengthways and press. Fold one of the raw edges into the middle and press. Repeat for the other raw edge.

3 Fold the sides to the middle and press again.

4 Using the walking foot, stitch along either side of the handle piece. Sewing along both edges adds extra strength to the handles. Repeat steps 2–4 for the other handle.

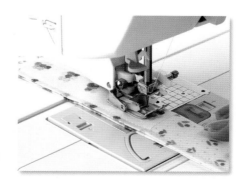

Finishing the bag

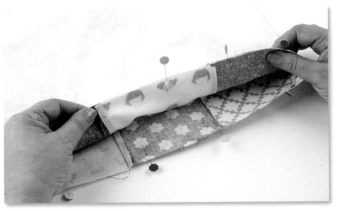

1   Turn the patchwork right side out and pin the handles in place 3in (7.5cm) from the edge of your bag. Remember that the handles need to hang down the outside of the patchwork. It is easier if you tack the handles in place before going any further.

2   Make sure that the lining is inside out, and the bag is right side out. Put the bag inside the lining so that they are right sides together. You must ensure that the handles are tucked between the lining and the outside fabric. If you stitch through the handles, the bag will not turn out correctly! Match up the edge seams and pin it all securely.

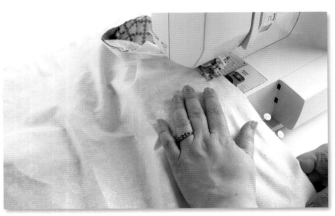

3   Sew all the way around the opening at the top – be careful as there are quite a few layers in places so take it slow. Your walking foot will be useful here too.

4   This is where the gap you left in the lining comes into its own. Carefully pull the whole bag the right way out through that hole. It will be tight, but just be patient and go slowly. Once it is all out, sew up the hole in the lining and tuck the lining back inside the bag. Press the bag.

5   Finish with a row of topstitching all the way around the top of the bag to give it a professional finish.

FRENCH BRAID TABLE RUNNER

This technique is a fun and fast way to create a stunning French braid for use as multiples in a quilt or singularly as a table runner. It is simple to construct but looks anything but! It is called a French braid because it resembles the braided hairstyle of the same name.

This table runner measures 62½in (159cm) long and 11½in (29cm) wide, but you can make it longer or shorter simply by adapting the number of strips you use.

You will need:

- Five fat eighths or a jelly roll (2½in (6.5cm) wide strips)
- Fat quarter of contrasting fabric
- 12in (30.5cm) of binding fabric
- Wadding to fit 66 x 15in (167.5 x 38cm), approx. 19¾in (50cm)
- 39½in (1m) of backing – this will need to be pieced unless you have extra wide backing, in which case you will only need 19¾in (50cm)

Cutting instructions

1   If you are using a jelly roll, you will already have 2½in (6.5cm) strips. If you are using fat eighths, you will need to cut four 2½in (6.5cm) wide strips from each of your five colours.

2   Cut your strips into 8½in (21.5cm) long pieces. These need to be kept in pairs when you cut them out.

3   From your contrasting fabric, cut 2½in (6.5cm) wide strips, and then cut these into 2½in (6.5cm) squares. You will need one square for each pair you have cut. To make this size table runner you will need twenty pairs of 8½ x 2½in (21.5 x 6.5cm) strips and twenty 2½in (6.5cm) squares.

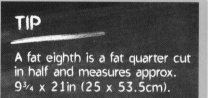

TIP

A fat eighth is a fat quarter cut in half and measures approx. 9¾ x 21in (25 x 53.5cm).

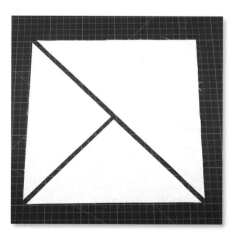

4   Cut a square from your contrasting fabric, measuring 9½in (24cm) square and cut it in half diagonally. Then cut one piece in half again to make two quarter square triangles (QSTs). Put the smaller triangles to one side for later.

Sewing instructions

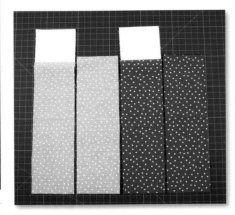

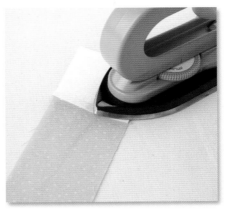

1   For each pair of 8½ x 2½in (21.5 x 6.5cm) strips, sew one of the contrasting squares to the end of one of them. Do not sew a square onto the other strip of the pair.

2   Press to the dark side (if possible) but keep the direction consistent because this will help to line up your intersections.

3   Take a pair of strips. Sew the shorter piece of the pair along one side of the large triangle. Make sure you line up the strip with the right-angled edge of the triangle. Press to the dark side.

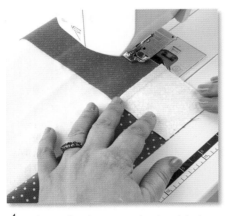

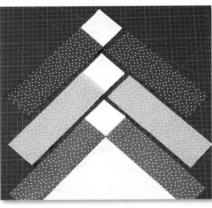

4   Then take the second strip with the attached square and sew that on the other side of the large triangle (right sides together). Make sure you have a good intersection, so pin if necessary. Again, press to the darker fabric.

5   Continue sewing the short piece on one side, and then the piece with the square on the other side. Always line up with the centre square, not the outside edges, as these edges will be trimmed away at the end.

6   Once your runner is the required length, take the two quarter square triangles (QSTs) you cut earlier and sew onto the 'pointy' end to square it off. Overlap the end of the triangle by about ¼in (0.6cm).

I am sewing the strips until the runner is the required length.

Here you can see the runner at the required length, with the two QSTs sewn onto the 'pointy' end to square it off.

7 Cut wadding and backing measuring 2in (5cm) wider than your table runner all the way around. You can use any of the layering methods covered on page 110 to attach the three layers together.

8 Quilt as desired, using any of the quilting methods covered on pages 111–119. In this project, I used my walking foot to 'stitch in the ditch' along the edges of the centre squares. I wanted the quilting to be invisible so I chose a fine matching thread (InvisaFil by WonderFil).

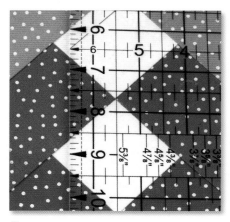

9 Measure 5½in (14cm) from the centre of the table runner and trim along the edges. The 5½in (14cm) line should go through the apex of each of the centre squares.

10 Bind as desired, using any of the binding methods covered on pages 120–124. Here, I used my walking foot to sew traditional binding around the edge of my table runner. To do this with your table runner, cut four 2½in (6.5cm) strips from your binding fabric, stitch together and complete the binding as instructed on pages 120–124.

TURNED FOUR-PATCH BED RUNNER

Who doesn't love a project that looks harder than it is? This bed runner is one of those projects!

To create this bed runner measuring 56½ × 16½in (143.5 × 42cm) we use fourteen blocks. All you need to make it longer or wider is more blocks.

You will need:

- A selection of fat quarters in contrasting colours – I have used eight different fabrics from my own 'Eastern Botanicals' range
- 19¾in (50cm) of binding fabric
- 39½in (1m) of backing fabric – this will need to be pieced unless you have extra wide backing where you will only need 19¾in (50cm)
- Wadding to fit 20 x 60in (51 x 152cm)

Cutting instructions

Cut six 5in (12.5cm) squares from four of your fabrics. Cut eight 5in (12.5cm) squares from the remaining four fabrics. You will need a total of fifty-six 5in (12.5cm) squares.

Eight different fabrics from my own 'Eastern Botanicals' range.

Choosing your blocks

Each block will use two different fabrics, so take two squares of each fabric and match them up with two squares of a different fabric, choosing combinations with interesting contrasts.

Sewing instructions

1   The basis of this block is a four patch – four squares sewn together. Select a pair and place the fabrics right sides together with raw edges meeting up. Pin if necessary and stitch along one side edge with a ¼in (0.6cm) seam allowance. Repeat with the other pair of squares, paying special attention if the fabrics have a directional design on them. Press the seams in opposite directions for each pair.

2   Orient the fabrics so that they are in opposite corners and sew the pairs together to create a four patch. We could stop there, and simply add more four patches until we have the correct size, but we have already done this with the bag on pages 28–33. So now we are going to take it up a gear!

3   Place your completed four patch on your cutting mat. Measure 1¼in (3cm) away from the centre seam line and cut.

4   Rotate the block (a rotating cutting mat is very useful, so maybe add this to your wish list!) and cut 1¼in (3cm) from the centre seam again. Continue rotating until you have cut all four sides.

5   Leaving the corner blocks as they are, rotate the rectangular sections so that they face the other direction.

Here is what I call the 'exploded' view – you can see from above how all the pieces have been moved into their correct positions, before they are sewn together.

6 Now we are going to sew the pieces back together again. This design may take a little manipulation of the seam allowances to get them pressed in opposite directions, because we have moved the pieces around. But it is worth a quick press to get nice intersections. Create a total of fourteen blocks using this method.

7 Sew the finished blocks into pairs, and then sew all seven pairs together to complete the bed runner. If you want to make it bigger, add more rows or simply use bigger squares to start with!

8 Layer the quilt. If you can get extra wide fabric for your backing, you will be able to create your back from one piece. If not, you will need to stitch two lengths together and press the connecting seam flat (or open).

9 Quilt as desired, using any of the quilting methods covered on pages 111–119. Here I used my walking foot to 'stitch in the ditch' along the outside of the squares. I wanted the quilting to be invisible so I chose a fine matching thread (InvisaFil by WonderFil).

10 Trim to size and bind as desired, using any of the binding methods covered on pages 120–124. Here I used my walking foot to sew traditional binding around the edge of my bed runner. For this I cut enough 2½in (6.5cm) wide fabric strips that once I stitched them together they made a piece approximately 150in (3.8m) long.

Here you can see the completed bed runner and the backing fabric used.

DISAPPEARING NINE-PATCH QUILT

This is a fabulous design and is the second pattern that I ever learned. Since then I must have made it a hundred times and it is my 'go to' pattern when I need a quilt in a hurry. It comes together quickly and looks much more complicated than it is. Everyone loves a quilt that looks harder than it is!

This design is perfect for showing off those feature fabrics; ones with a strong print design that are just too gorgeous to cut up into smaller bits. Here I have used some precious hand-printed fabrics from my trip to India.

The design is called 'disappearing' nine patch because once you have cut up your block, you cannot see the original nine patch any more (it has disappeared).

This quilt measures 54 x 72in (137 x 183cm).

You will need:

- 19¾in (50cm) of four feature fabrics – big patterns are good
- 59in (1.5m) of coordinating fabric
- 19¾in (50cm) of contrasting fabric
- 19¾in (50cm) of fabric for binding
- Wadding and backing to fit

Cutting instructions

You will make twelve blocks in total. If you want to make the quilt bigger, simply add more blocks. You will need to cut a lot of squares the same size, so make it easier by folding the fabric pieces in half so that the selvedge edges are matched up and cut strips measuring 6½in (16.5cm) long. Then cut the 6½in (16.5cm) squares from the strips. You will get six squares from each strip, and having the fabric strips folded means you can speed up the process by cutting two at a time.

To make this size you will need to cut:

- Twelve pieces of the contrasting fabric, measuring 6½in (16.5cm) square
- Forty-eight pieces of the coordinating fabric, measuring 6½in (16.5cm) square
- Twelve pieces of each of your four focal feature fabrics, measuring 6½in (16.5cm) square

Sewing instructions

If your fabrics are directional, make sure that the top left and bottom right squares are the correct way up. The other two squares need to be placed with the design upside down (rotated).

1 Place two squares right sides together and sew down one side with a ¼in (0.6cm) seam allowance. Add another square to make a row of three.

2 Press seams to the darker of the fabrics and create a total of three rows. Sew the three rows together to make a nine-patch block.

Here you can see the seams pressed to the dark side.

3 Cut the nine-patch block in half horizontally and vertically. If you rotate your mat between cuts you won't need to keep lining up the cut blocks.

4 Turn the two opposite squares (top right and bottom left) by 180°. This is where your nine patch 'disappears'.

5 Sew it all back together and you now have your completed nine patch.

6 Make twelve nine-patch blocks for this size quilt and sew them into rows of three blocks. Stitch the four rows together to make the quilt.

7 Layer and quilt as desired, using any of the quilting methods covered on pages 111–119. I used my walking foot to echo the seam line along the outside of the plain fabric area. I wanted the quilting to be a feature, so I chose a thicker thread (Spagetti™ 12wt/3ply Egyptian Cotton by WonderFil) to make the quilting more visible.

8 Trim to size, then bind as desired, using any of the binding methods covered on pages 120–124. I used my walking foot to sew traditional binding around the edge of the quilt. For this I cut seven fabric strips 2½in (6.5cm) wide to go all the way round my quilt.

Echo quilting.

Choosing your nine-patch colours

This fantastic block can create many different looks for a quilt. Simply by varying the number and position of the colours you use in the nine patch, you can alter how your quilt looks.

Nine block

If you choose three colours for your block, with the same fabric in all four corners…

Finished quilt

…the rotated quilt will look like this:

If you choose four different colours for each corner of your block…

…the rotated quilt will look like this:

If you select nine different colours in all your blocks…

…the rotated quilt will look like this:

If all the squares are different, but all the blocks are the same throughout the quilt…

…the rotated quilt will look like this:

SNOWBALL PILLOWCASE

You will need:
- Four fat quarters of fabric (one needs to be a contrasting fabric to the others)
- 29½in (75cm) of fabric for the border and for backing the pillowcase

This is a nice project to complete this section, because it takes us from squares into triangles which we will be exploring more in the next section. However, this is a bit of a helpful cheat, because no triangles were cut for this project – it is all about the squares!

This pattern is called a snowball block because it is an optical illusion designed to resemble circles from a distance. Luckily, these patterns are far simpler than they look. The snowball block is a wonderful and versatile quilt block for beginners.

This pattern will fit a standard pillowcase – 20 × 26in (51 × 66cm) – but you can vary it to fit different sizes by adding more blocks or adjusting the size of the borders.

Cutting instructions

1 Cut forty-eight 2in (5cm) squares from the contrasting fat quarter of fabric.

2 Cut four 6½in (16.5cm) squares from each of your three feature fabrics (twelve squares in total). You will get three squares per strip, so cut one strip and a single square to get the most out of your fabric.

Sum:
4 x 3 = 12

Sewing instructions

1 Take a pencil or water-soluble marker and draw a line diagonally across the centre of the small squares on the back of the fabric.

2 Take one of your large squares and place on your cutting mat right side (fabric side) up and pin the marked squares fabric side down in all corners, making sure the diagonal lines you drew do not point to the corners.

3 Stitch along the drawn line on each of the corners.

4 Trim ¼in (0.6cm) past the sewn line, cutting off the corners of the square. Discard the trimmed pieces.

5 It is easier to put the blocks together if you press the seams in opposite directions, but for now press all four corners open.

6 Lay out your blocks into three rows of four blocks. It is useful to press the angled seams on each of the blocks in opposite directions. This means that when you put two of your blocks together, the seams on your snowball edges will lock together in the same way we have seen in the earlier projects. This makes it far easier to get a good result and line up the little triangle edges of your snowball.

The front.

The back.

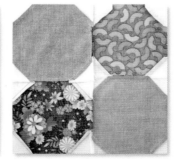

7 Sew each row together, then sew the rows together to create the centre of your pillowcase.

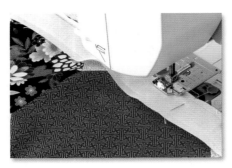
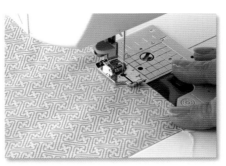
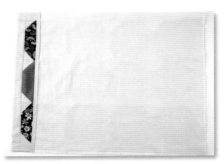

8 Cut three 1½in (3.5cm) wide strips from your border fabric. Take one of the strips and cut in half. Sew along the shorter edges of your pillowcase front. Press and trim the ends straight. Sew each of the other strips to the long sides of the pillowcase, then press and trim. At this point you can choose whether to quilt your pillowcase top. For this one I decided not to. If you wish, baste the wadding onto the back of your pillowcase front and quilt as desired.

9 Cut one piece from your pillowcase back fabric measuring 20½ × 24½in (52 × 62cm) and a second piece measuring 20½ × 8½in (52 × 21.5cm). Along the short edge of one of your fabric pieces, make a fold measuring ¼in (0.6cm) and press it flat. Then fold it over again and press that flat to create a neat edge. Sew this down with a line of topstitching. Repeat this with the second piece. These will create neat edges for the backing.

10 Now it is time to complete your pillowcase. Lay the front of your pillowcase right side up on your work surface. Lay the larger piece of the backing fabric right side down with the topstitched edge towards the middle of the pillowcase, lining up the raw edges.

DEFINITION

Topstitching means that you sew a row of continuous stitches on the top of the fabric as a decorative feature.

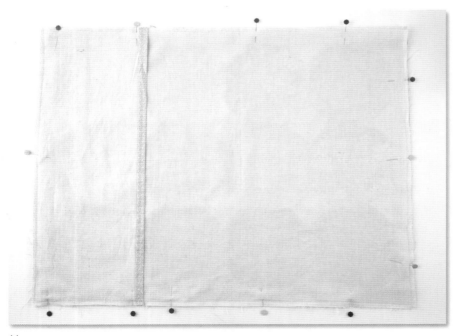

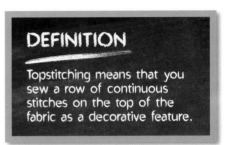

12 If you have quilted the pillowcase front, use your walking foot to deal with the extra bulk and prevent the fabrics slipping. Sew all the way around the outside of the pillowcase with a ¼in (0.6cm) seam allowance. Snip the fabric from the corners of the pillowcase to reduce bulk, being careful not to cut your stitches. Now turn your pillowcase through the opening and press.

11 Place the second piece on top. Pin all the way around the outside of the pillowcase. There should be an overlap of the backing so that the pillowcase can expand when the pillow is placed inside.

TRIANGLES

You have now mastered the square, and hopefully you are creating beautiful
intersections in your blocks by pressing the seams in opposite directions.
Now it is time to move on to the next step: triangles.

HALF SQUARE TRIANGLES

The half square triangle (HST) is a hugely popular block because it is just so versatile, and can be used in traditional and non-traditional designs. It is also easy to create and moves you on nicely from the squares you were playing with in the previous section. Plus, mastering the HST makes a novice quilter look clever!

There are two methods for creating half square triangles: the first is based on squares and the second uses a right-angled triangle ruler. You can use either method, to suit your tools or your mood!

Method 1: Square method

Cut two squares of fabric ⅞in (2cm) larger than you want the finished block. I would choose to round up to 1in (2.5cm) and then trim it square later. So if you want a 6in (15cm) block, cut a 7in (18cm) square.

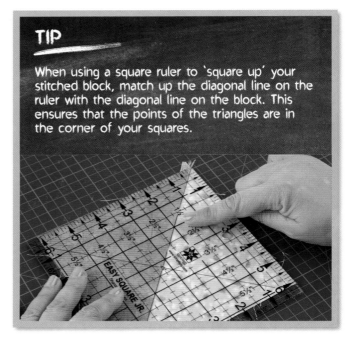

TIP

When using a square ruler to 'square up' your stitched block, match up the diagonal line on the ruler with the diagonal line on the block. This ensures that the points of the triangles are in the corner of your squares.

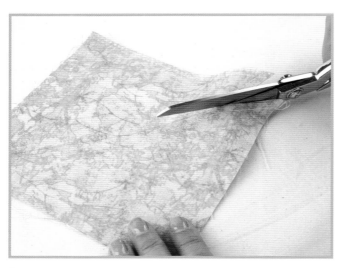

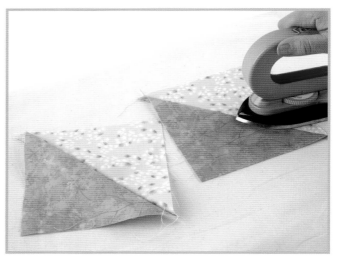

1　Take a pencil or water-soluble marker and draw a line on the back of the fabric diagonally across the centre of the lighter fabric square. Put the two squares right sides together and pin them. Stitch ¼in (0.6cm) away from both sides of the line, then cut along the line.

2　Open out the two halves and press to the darker fabric. If you cut your square larger, you can now trim your block to the correct size using a square ruler. You now have two HSTs.

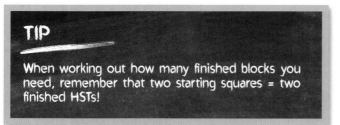

TIP

When working out how many finished blocks you need, remember that two starting squares = two finished HSTs!

50

Method 2: Ruler method

If you have an Easy Angle or right-angled triangle ruler this makes it all very easy! In this example we will create 6in (15cm) finished squares. You will need to add a total of ½in (1cm) for the seam allowance – ¼in (0.6cm) for each edge.

Take the two colours that you want to make your HSTs from and place the fabrics right sides together. It is easier to cut two layers at once as they will come out ready to sew together!

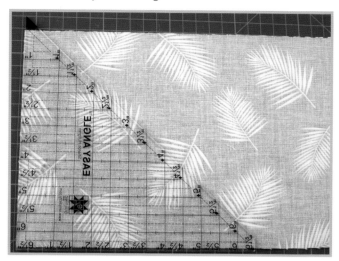

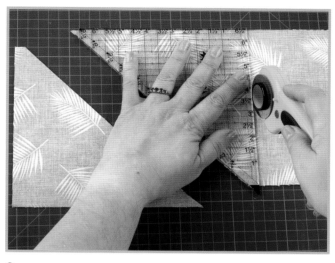

1   Cut two 6½in (16.5cm) strips of the two colours. Place your Easy Angle triangle so that the black tip lies beyond the strip. The bottom of the strip should run along the 6½in (16.5cm) line on the Easy Angle. The ruler is flipped when it is used to cut triangles, so sometimes the text will appear backwards. Now cut up the diagonal line to create a pair of triangles.

2   Flip the ruler and cut up the square edge to cut the next set.

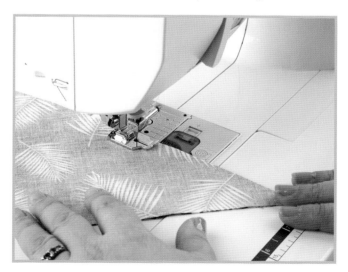

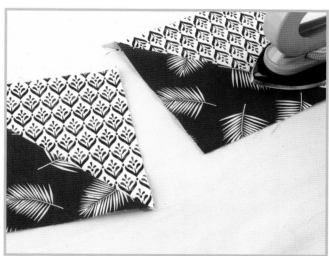

3   Sew down the diagonal line using a ¼in (0.6cm) seam allowance.

4   Open the two halves and press the two triangles out to show the HST. Press the seams towards the darker of the fabric triangles.

TIP

Do not press your triangles between cutting and stitching, as this can stretch the bias cut diagonal edge.

HALF SQUARE TRIANGLE BEDSPREAD

What can we do now we know how to make half square triangles (HST)? The HST on its own makes a great quilt design. The finished bedspread is 59in (1.5m) square.

You will need:

- 19¾in (50cm) of four fabrics, plus an extra 29½in (75cm) of one of these for your border fabric
- 59in (1.5m) of contrasting fabric
- 19¾in (50cm) for binding
- 3¼yd (3m) of backing fabric (this will need to be pieced unless you have extra wide backing where you will only need 59in (1.5m)
- Wadding to fit 64 x 64in (162.5 x 162.5cm)

Variation

If you are using the square method for making your blocks (see page 50), you could use pre-cut squares from a charm pack (5in (12.5cm) squares) or a layer cake (10in (25.5cm) squares) to change the size of the project. This will also make it quicker to put together. 5in (12.5cm) squares will make finished blocks 4in (10cm) wide and the 10in (25.5cm) squares will make finished blocks 9in (22.5cm) wide. Varying the size of the blocks will result in a different sized finished quilt.

Cutting instructions

These HST blocks finish at 6in (15cm) square and there are sixty-four blocks in total.

Square method (see page 50) Cut thirty-two 6⅞in (17.5cm) squares of the contrasting fabric, and eight 6⅞in (17.5cm) from each of your four fabrics. You might find it easier to round up to 7in (18cm).

Ruler method (see page 51) Cut 6½in (16.5cm) wide strips and cut a total of sixty-four triangles from the contrasting fabric, and sixteen triangles from each of your four fabrics.

Sewing instructions

1 Follow the instructions for whichever method you prefer and make sixty-four HST blocks, each with one half as the contrasting fabric. Press the diagonal seam away from the contrast for consistency. I like to start my quilts from the top right corner and sew the rows together as I go. You may like to work differently, but you need to pay close attention to the layout for this design. Begin by laying out your blocks in rows. There are other layouts you could follow on page 57.

2 Sew the blocks together a row at a time. Take the first two squares and lay them right sides together (printed sides) and sew using a ¼in (0.6cm) seam allowance along one side. Then add the next square and sew until you have eight blocks. Continue until you have finished the whole row. Press all the block seams in one direction.

3 Sew the next row in the same way, but press the seams in the opposite direction to the first row. Continue until all eight rows are sewn and pressed.

4 Now take the first and second rows and place them right sides together, matching up the squares. Because you have pressed the seams in opposite directions, they should snuggle into each other making them match up more easily. It can be useful to pin each intersecting point, and both ends of the row. After sewing together, open up the rows and press the seams in one direction.

5 Continue in the same way until all your rows are sewn together and pressed.

Adding borders to this design not only makes it slightly larger, I think it really finishes the design beautifully.

You will need to piece strips together to create the borders.

6   For the inner border, choose one of the fabrics used for the blocks (just not the contrasting fabric). Cut enough strips measuring 1½in (4cm) wide to make four border pieces each measuring approximately 50in (127cm) long. Pin two of the narrow border strips to the sides and sew each one in place. Press the seams out to the border and trim the ends square. Repeat with the top and bottom of the quilt.

7   For the outer border, select the fabric that you have chosen for the wide border. Cut six strips measuring 4½in (11.5cm) wide. Sew two pieces of the 4½in (11.5cm) wide border material together to make a long piece. Pin the strips to the sides and sew each one in place. Press the seams out to the border and trim the ends square. Repeat for the top and bottom borders. Pin them in place and sew. Press the seams out to the border and trim the ends square.

8   Layer the quilt. If you can get extra wide fabric for your backing, you will be able to create your back from one piece. If not, you will need to stitch two lengths together and press the connecting seam flat (or open).

Above: You can see how to piece your strips together to create the borders.

Below: Here you can see the lovely effect given by adding a border.

9 Quilt as desired, using any of the quilting methods covered on pages 111–119. Here I used my walking foot to 'stitch in the ditch' along the outside of the triangles. I wanted the quilting to be invisible so I chose a fine matching thread (InvisaFil by WonderFil). How you choose to quilt this piece is really up to you – you can use any style you like. The contrasting areas provide a gorgeous space for practising some free-motion quilting and the main shape leaves scope for straight line quilting around it. You can of course choose to hand quilt it too.

10 Trim to size, then bind as desired, using any of the binding methods covered on pages 120–124. Here I used my walking foot to sew traditional binding around the edge. For this I cut enough 2½in (6.5cm) wide fabric strips that once I stitched them together they made a piece approximately 250in (6.4m) long.

Close-up of quilting: you can barely see it because it is in the ditch (between the diagonal blocks).

Opposite: A bedspread can keep you warm, but will also really finish off the appearance of a room.

Alternative layouts

There are a number of other ways you can lay out these same blocks to give a different look:

Pinwheel variation.

Split chevron.

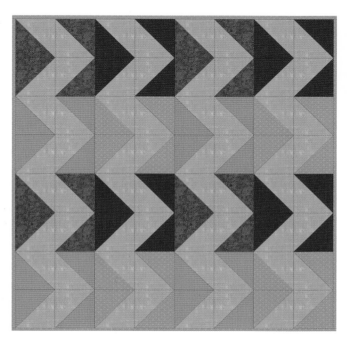

Chevron.

JACOB'S LADDER QUILT

This pattern uses jelly roll strips and a couple of fat quarters to make a quick and easy quilt and is perfect for beginners. It combines the squares that you mastered in the previous section, and the triangles in this one. We will also add a couple of borders as well as a flange border. The binding I have chosen for this quilt is also great fun!

This pattern uses half square triangles (HSTs) and four-patch blocks to make this interesting quilt.

This version is made up of nine blocks and finishes at 48in (122cm) including borders. To make a larger quilt, just keep adding blocks!

You will need:

- Twenty-four strips cut from fat quarters, or twelve jelly roll strips – I have used the fat quarters from the 'Kimono' range designed by Stuart Hillard
- 39½in (1m) of background fabric for the blocks
- 69in (1.75m) of contrasting fabric for the blocks and the outer border
- If you wish to add the red flange border and bordered binding you will need 19¾in (50cm) of the red contrasting fabric and 19¾in (50cm) of white fabric. If you are using a standard binding you will just need 19¾in (50cm) of the white fabric

Cutting instructions for HST block

These HST blocks finish at 4in (10cm) square and there are thirty-six blocks in total.

Square method (see page 50) Cut eighteen 4⅞in (12.5cm) squares of the background fabric, and eighteen 4⅞in (12.5cm) of your contrasting fabric. You might find it easier to round up to 5in (12.5cm).

Ruler method (see page 51) Cut 4½in (11.5cm) wide strips and cut a total of thirty-six triangles from the background fabric, and thirty-six triangles from the contrasting fabric.

Cutting instructions for four-patch block

Cut a total of twenty-four 2½in (6.5cm) wide strips from your fat quarters or use twelve fat quarter strips.

Sewing instructions for HST block

1   Use your preferred method to create thirty-six sets of HSTs.

2   Check the finished size of each square is 4½in (11.5cm) and trim if necessary.

Sewing instructions for four-patch block

Make forty-five four-patch blocks as follows:

1   The quickest method of making the squares is to quick piece the 2½in (6.5cm) wide strips into pairs.

2   Cut the pairs down to 2½in (6.5cm) long pieces.

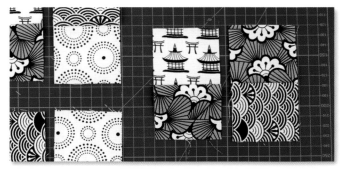

3   Press the seams to the dark side. Then sew two of the pieces together into a square. Check the finished size of each square is 4½in (11.5cm) and trim if necessary.

4   Make forty-five mixed sets (you will need five per block).

Assembling the block

Each 12in (30.5cm) finished block uses four HSTs and five four-patch blocks.

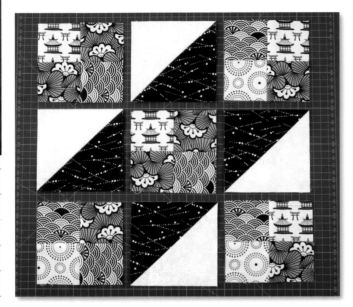

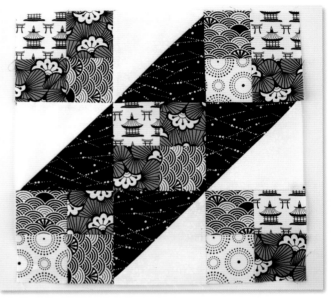

1 Sew three blocks together in three rows as shown. It is useful to lay out each block prior to sewing the rows together because it is easy to accidentally sew the half square triangles upside down! Pay attention to the tips of the triangles because it is obvious if you cut one off! Press the seams in opposite directions.

2 Sew each of the three rows and then sew them together to make your completed block and press the seams in opposite directions. Make nine of these blocks in total.

3 Set the blocks into three rows of three blocks (see alternative layout options on page 63). Place the first two blocks right sides together and pin the intersections together carefully. This is where pressing can help lock those seams together. Sew together and continue until you have sewn all the rows. Now sew the rows together to complete the centre of your quilt.

Borders

Borders not only make your quilt larger without much effort, but they can really add to the design of your quilt. For this sample, I have added three extra borders (two traditional borders and a flange border). You will need to piece strips together to create some of the borders.

I have selected a red fabric for the flange border, in sharp contrast to all the blue and white in the quilt.

DEFINITION

A flange border is a border that is only held down on one side with the raw edges embedded in the seam. It looks interesting and is a good way of including a very thin line of colour in your design.

1 For the white inner border, cut four strips measuring 1½in (4cm) wide and at least 38in (96.5cm) long. Pin two of the narrow border strips to the sides of your quilt and sew each one in place. Press the seams out to the border and trim the ends square. Repeat with the top and bottom of the quilt.

2   To make a flange border, cut four strips each measuring 1in (2.5cm) wide and at least 38in (96.5cm) long. Fold each strip in half along its length with the wrong sides of the fabric together (print side out) and press. Pin the raw edges of the strip to the edge of the quilt and stitch in place with a ⅛in (0.25cm) seam allowance. These stitches will be hidden by the next border when it is added. Press the flange flat and repeat for all four borders.

4   Sew three pieces of the 5in (12.5cm) wide border material together to make a long piece. Cut it in half to make two long pieces. Pin each to the remaining sides of the quilt and sew. Press the seams out to the border and trim the ends square.

5   Layer the quilt. If you can get extra wide fabric for your backing, you will be able to create your back from one piece. If not, you will need to stitch two lengths together and press the connecting seam flat (or open).

3   For the outer border, cut five strips measuring 5in (12.5cm) wide. Pin two of the strips to the sides and sew each one in place, making sure that the flange border is captured between the first and second border.

6   Quilt as desired and trim to size, then bind using any of the binding methods covered on pages 120–124. You will need to make your binding at least 17½ft (5.3m) long. I used the bordered binding technique to add a little more red to my design. From white binding fabric cut strips measuring 1¼in (3cm) wide and from the red cut 1¾in (4.5cm) wide strips. I have used the red for the wider strip and this becomes the inner border. Sew the strips together with a ¼in (0.6cm) seam allowance each and press the raw edges together. This is where the overlap of the red is created. See page 123 for how to attach it.

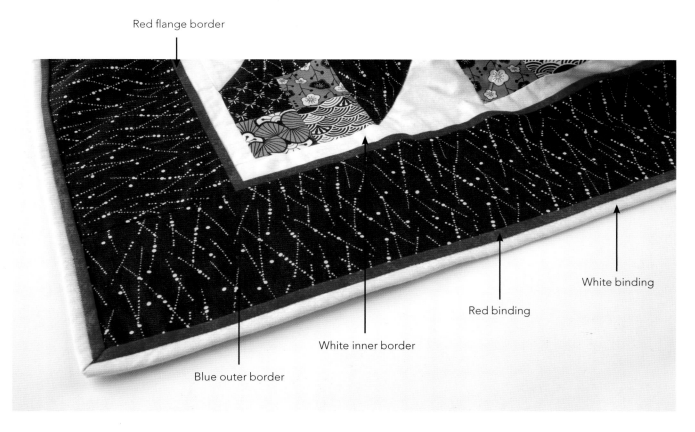

Red flange border

White binding

Red binding

White inner border

Blue outer border

Alternative layouts

Offset diamond.

Diagonals.

Crosses.

OHIO STAR CUSHION COVER

You will need:
- A fat quarter of three fabrics
- 18in (45.5cm) cushion pad

Now you have mastered the HST, you can take it further and create a quarter square triangle (QST) for this fabulous traditional block. Ohio star on point is the name of the centre panel block on this cushion cover. 'On point' means that the block is set in the quilt on an angle and requires the addition of triangles to the square block.

This fun and easy cover will have you making QSTs in a whizz – and it will make a great gift for friends and family.

The finished cushion cover measures 18in (45.5cm) square.

Method one

bias stretch

Method two

bias stretch

I use method one for making the QSTs, so the bias stretch is in the centre of the block.

With the QST, we do not generally use HST method 2 (the ruler method, see page 51) for cutting our triangles. The reason for this is that the biased (stretchy) edge of the triangle will now be on the outside of the block, making squaring up very tricky! Think of trying to sew through jelly! Using the square method (see page 50) will keep the diagonal bias cut edges in the centre of the block where they belong. The first few steps in this project will be familiar if you have used the square method for your HST.

To make a QST, you need to take the finished block measurement and add 1¼in (3cm) to it as a seam allowance. To make the correct sized centre for the cushion cover, we will be working with 4¼in (11cm) finished blocks, so adding 1¼in (3cm) to that measurement gives us a cutting size of 5½in (14cm).

Cutting instructions

1 Cut two 5½in (14cm) squares from the blue fabric; one from the pink fabric and one from the floral fabric.

2 Cut one 4¾in (12cm) square of pink fabric, and four from blue fabric. You can vary the look of the block by substituting the blue fabric with the floral fabric, as in the main image shown opposite.

3 Cut two 10in (25.5cm) squares from the blue fabric.

Sewing instructions

First, make your HSTs:

1 Using a pencil or water-soluble marker, lightly draw a diagonal line across the centre of the two 5½in (14cm) blue fabric squares. Pair up each of the blue squares with a coloured square (one with a pink square and one with a floral square) and pin them right sides together.

2 Stitch ¼in (0.6cm) on either side of the drawn line.

3 Cut along the drawn line. Now open the two halves and press to show the HST. Press the seams towards the darker of the fabric triangles.

4 You now have two HSTs. Repeat with the other pair to make four sets.

To make your HSTs into QSTs, follow these steps:

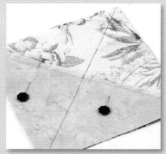

1 Take one pink HST and one floral HST and place them right sides together with the blue fabric touching a different colour. Make sure that the diagonal seams match up.

2 Using a pencil or water-soluble marker, draw a line from corner to corner, bisecting the HST seam. Stitch a scant ¼in (0.6cm) away from both sides of the line.

3 Cut along the line.

4 Open out the two halves and press. You now have two QSTs. Repeat with the other pairs to make four sets. Trim to 4¾in (12cm).

Making up the block

1 Lay out the 4¾in (12cm) squares with the QST as shown opposite.

2 Sew the rows together. For the first and the third row, press the seams to the outside squares. For the second row, press the seams into the centre block. This will make it easier to line up the seams. Sew all the rows together to complete the Ohio star.

Finishing the central block

Cut the 10in (25.5cm) blue squares in half diagonally to make four large triangles. Pin to one corner of the Ohio star, making sure it is centrally placed. There will be a little bit of fabric overlapping the ends, but do not worry. Stitch in place and press. Repeat with the opposite side of your block. Attach the final two triangles and your central block is completed. Trim to 18½in (47cm) square.

The finished central block.

Envelope backing for a cushion cover

This is a simple method for creating a neat envelope backing for your cushion cover.

1   Cut two pieces of your backing fabric measuring the width of your cushion front by approximately two-thirds of the length of your cushion front. For example, a 12in (30.5cm) cushion would use two pieces measuring 12 × 8in (30.5 × 20.5cm). This is so that the overlap hides the cushion pad once it is inserted.

2   Along the long edge of one of your fabric pieces, make a fold measuring ¼in (0.6cm) and press it flat. Then fold it over again and press that flat to create a neat edge. Sew this down with a line of topstitching (continuous stitches on the top of the fabric as a decorative feature).

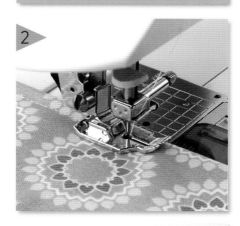

3   Repeat this with the second piece. This will create neat edges for the envelope backing.

4   To complete your cushion cover, lay the front of your cushion cover right side up on your work surface. Lay one piece of the background fabric right side down with the topstitched edge across the middle of the cushion cover.

5   Place the second piece on top. Pin all the way around the outside of the cushion. There should be an overlap of the backing in the middle so that the cover can expand when the pad is placed inside.

6   Sew all the way around the outside of the cover with a ¼in (0.6cm) seam allowance. Snip the fabric from the corners of the cushion cover to reduce bulk, being careful not to cut your stitches. Now turn your cover through the opening and press.

7   Insert a suitable cushion pad, step back and admire your handiwork.

FLYING GEESE

Flying geese are rectangular patchwork quilting blocks that are twice as long as they are high. Each one has a right-angled triangle at its centre and smaller triangles flank either side of the peak. Think of the centre triangle as the formation that geese fly in, and the side triangles as the 'sky'. Accurate measuring is vital for consistent blocks.

There are three methods for creating flying geese blocks and I will look at each one in turn and then refer back to them. You can choose which one you want to use based on the project you have planned.

The first method (one geese) can give very accurate flying geese as long as you stitch along the straight lines. It is a great method if you want a lot of different coloured geese because you can make them individually.

However, some people do not like this method because of the waste involved – you are cutting off those little triangle edges. Nevertheless, you could keep these and stitch them together to make teeny HSTs to use in a later project.

METHOD ONE
One geese method: Cutting instructions

1 For the geese, cut a rectangle that's ½in (1.5cm) larger than the finished size of your flying geese. For example, cut a rectangle that measures 3½ x 6½in (8.5 x 16.5cm) to make a 3 x 6in (7.5 x 15cm) block.

2 For the 'sky', cut two small squares that are ½in (1.5cm) larger than the finished height of your flying block. For example, cut two squares that measure 3½in (8.5cm) square to complete a 3 x 6in (7.5 x 15cm) block.

COMMON SIZES FOR FLYING GEESE BLOCKS WITH THE ONE GEESE METHOD

2 x 4in (5 x 10cm) finished block:
- Cut 2½ x 4½in (6.5 x 11.5cm) rectangle from the geese fabric.
- Cut two 2½in (6.5cm) squares from the sky fabric.

3 x 6in (7.5 x 15cm) finished block:
- Cut 3½ x 6½in (8.5 x 16.5cm) rectangle from the geese fabric.
- Cut two 3½in (8.5cm) squares from the sky fabric.

4 x 8in (10 x 20.5cm) finished block:
- Cut 4½ x 8½in (11.5 x 21.5cm) rectangle from the geese fabric.
- Cut two 4½in (11.5cm) squares from the sky fabric.

5 x 10in (12.5 x 25.5cm) finished block:
- Cut 5½ x 10½in (14 x 26.5cm) rectangle from the geese fabric.
- Cut two 5½in (14cm) squares from the sky fabric.

Sewing instructions

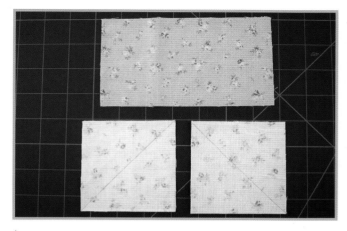

1 Using an erasable pen, draw a line diagonally from corner to corner on the reverse side of the two small squares.

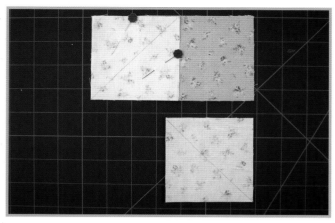

2 Pin one of the squares on the rectangle, right sides (pattern sides) together. The drawn line should point to the centre of the rectangle.

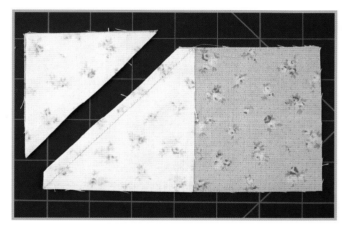

3 Sew a seam along the drawn line. Cut ¼in (0.6cm) from the drawn line.

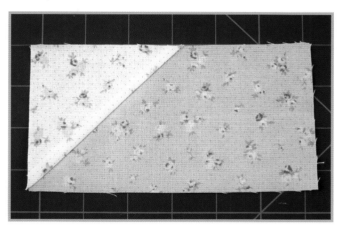

4 Press the triangle back.

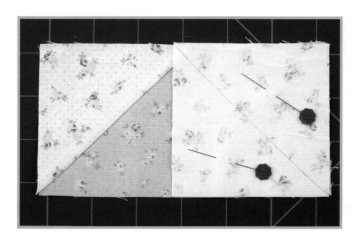

5 Pin the other square on the other corner and sew as before.

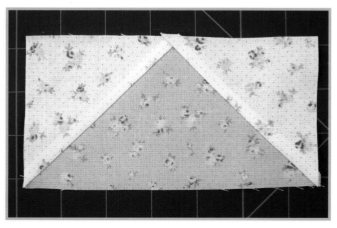

6 Cut and press open – you now have a flying geese block.

METHOD TWO
Ruler method

Using a ruler is a popular method for creating flying geese as the blocks are quick to cut and there is no maths involved.

The rulers work with strips and they will often tell you what sizes you need to be cutting for your block. The strips for the 'geese' and the 'sky' fabrics will be the same width, therefore you can cut your strips in multiples quickly too.

The basic measurement for this method is that you cut your strips based on the finished height of the block – so you simply add ½in (1.5cm). The steps below will create 3 x 6in (7.5 x 15cm) blocks.

WHY?

The reason why we don't simply cut our triangles using a standard right-angled triangle ruler is that we need to pay attention to the direction of the bias stretch in our triangle. We want the stretchy edges to be stitched together within the block, and the stable grain edge to be on the outside of the block. This makes it so much easier to put together.

Cutting instructions

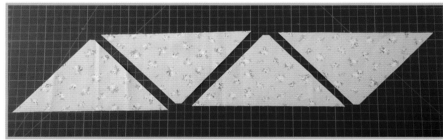

Here are the four triangles cut from the geese fabric.

1   Cut a 3½in (8.5cm) wide strip from the geese fabric. Use the companion angle ruler to cut one triangle per block.

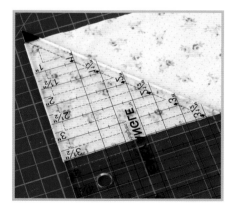

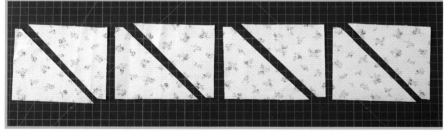

Here are the eight triangles cut from the sky fabric.

2   Cut a 3½in (8.5cm) wide strip from the sky fabric. Use the Easy Angle ruler to cut two corner triangles per block.

COMMON SIZES FOR FLYING GEESE BLOCKS WITH THE RULER METHOD

2 x 4in (5 x 10cm) finished block:
- Cut 2½in (6.5cm) wide strip from the geese fabric.
- Cut 2½in (6.5cm) wide strip from the sky fabric.

3 x 6in (7.5 x 15cm) finished block:
- Cut 3½in (8.5cm) wide strip from the geese fabric.
- Cut 3½in (8.5cm) wide strip from the sky fabric.

4 x 8in (10 x 20.5cm) finished block:
- Cut 4½in (11.5cm) wide strip from the geese fabric.
- Cut 4½in (11.5cm) wide strip from the sky fabric.

5 x 10in (12.5 x 25.5cm) finished block:
- Cut 5½in (14cm) wide strip from the geese fabric.
- Cut 5½in (14cm) wide strip from the sky fabric.

Sewing instructions

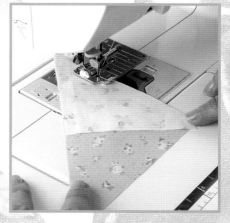  

1   Once you have cut out two sky pieces for every geese triangle, place one of the sky pieces on to the geese and stitch along the slope using a ¼in (0.6cm) seam allowance.

2   Open and press to the sky. Repeat with the other side.

3   Press and your block is completed.

METHOD THREE
Four geese method

This is often called the 'no waste method' because you are making four geese at one time with no fabric waste. If you have lots to make it feels very quick. However, you must pay attention to your stitch lines or the resulting flying geese may become a little wobbly. For this method, you will need to add 1¼in (3cm) to the width of your geese, and ⅞in (2cm) to the height.

Cutting instructions

1   For the geese, cut a square 1¼in (3cm) larger than the finished width of your flying geese. For example, cut a square that measures 7¼ x 7¼in (18.5 x 18.5cm) to make a 3 x 6in (7.5 x 15cm) block.

2   For the 'sky', cut four small squares that are ⅞in (2cm) larger than the finished height of your flying block. For example, cut four squares that measure 3⅞ x 3⅞in (10 x 10cm) to complete a 3 x 6in (7.5 x 15cm) block.

COMMON SIZES FOR FLYING GEESE BLOCKS WITH THE FOUR GEESE METHOD

2 x 4in (5 x 10cm) finished block:
- Cut one 5¼in (13.5cm) square from the geese fabric.
- Cut four 2⅞in (7.5cm) squares from the sky fabric.

3 x 6in (7.5 x 15cm) finished block:
- Cut one 7¼in (18.5cm) square from the geese fabric.
- Cut four 3⅞in (10cm) squares from the sky fabric.

4 x 8in (10 x 20.5cm) finished block:
- Cut one 9¼in (23.5cm) square from the geese fabric.
- Cut four 4⅞in (12.5cm) squares from the sky fabric.

5 x 10in (12.5 x 25.5cm) finished block:
- Cut one 11¼in (28.5cm) square from the geese fabric.
- Cut four 5⅞in (15cm) squares from the sky fabric.

Sewing instructions

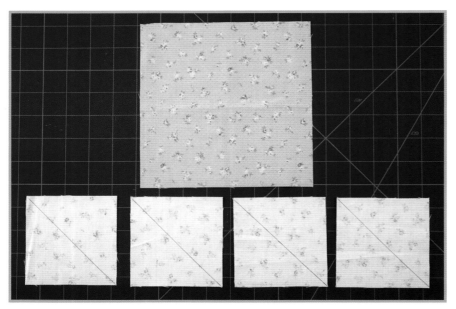

1   Using an erasable pen, draw a line diagonally from corner to corner on the reverse side of the four small squares.

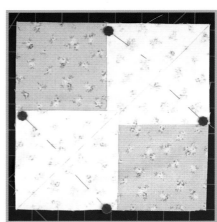

2   Pin two small squares on the large square, right sides together and in opposite corners. The drawn lines should line up and the small squares overlap in the middle.

3 Sew two seams, each a scant ¼in (0.6cm) away from the marked lines. Cut along the drawn line.

4 Press the triangles in each unit open.

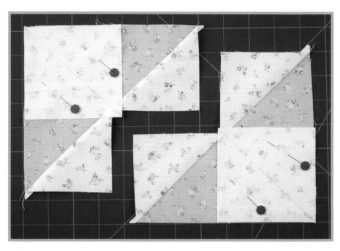

5 Place one of the small squares in the corner of each unit, right sides together, with the drawn line pointing into the peak. Sew two seams, each a scant ¼in (0.6cm) away from the marked lines – just as you did for the first squares.

6 Cut along the drawn line.

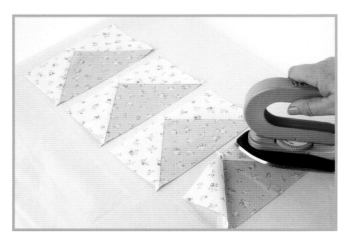

7 Press the triangles in each unit open to create four flying geese blocks. Repeat to make as many flying geese as needed.

FLYING SOUTH FOR THE WINTER WALL HANGING

This is a very striking wall hanging using flying geese blocks. It is a simple project that goes together quickly, because much of the design is background. I also decided to use prairie points in the binding to mirror the flying geese as they fly south.

The finished project measures 34½ × 47½in (87.5 × 120.5cm).

You will need:

- Four fat quarters
- 39½in (1m) of contrasting fabric
- 19¾in (50cm) of border fabric – I used an ombre style but any co-ordinating fabric will work
- 29½in (75cm) of white fabric for binding and prairie points

Cutting instructions

The flying geese used here have a finished measurement of 3 × 6in (7.5 × 15cm) and you need twenty-four of them. There are three different methods you can use, detailed on pages 68–73.

One geese method Cut twenty-four 3½ × 6½in (8.5 × 16.5cm) rectangles from the blue fabrics and forty-eight 3½in (8.5cm) squares from the background fabric.

Ruler method Cut twenty-four 3½ × 6½in (8.5 × 16.5cm) rectangles from a 3½in (8.5cm) strip of the blue fabrics and forty-eight 3½in (8.5cm) triangles from a 3½in (8.5cm) strip of the background fabric.

Four geese method If you are keeping the colours as they are in the sample this is not an appropriate method because you want six from each colour and this method will yield four or eight geese.

In addition, you will need to cut six squares measuring 5½in (14cm) and six squares measuring 9½in (24cm) from the background fabric. Cut all the squares in half diagonally to create right-angled triangles.

Cut four strips measuring 4½in (11.5cm) wide from the border fabric.

For the prairie points, cut two strips of fabric 6in (15cm) wide, and then cut twelve 6in (15cm) squares from the strips.

In this detail from the finished piece opposite, you can see the free-motion quilting – done in feather shapes.

In this detail from the finished piece opposite, you can see the prairie points in the binding.

Sewing instructions

1 Follow your chosen method (see pages 68–73) to make a total of twenty-four geese. Arrange them into sets of four.

2 Place a pair right sides together with the pointed end of one touching the wide end of the next and stitch together with a ¼in (0.6cm) seam allowance.

3 Make sure you stitch on the point, where the stitching for the geese meets in a right angle, not through it as this will cut the tip off.

4 Your stitches will form a star.

5 Sew a strip of four together and then stitch one of the 5½in (14cm) triangles at each of the short ends. Press the seams to the background.

6 Take one of the 9½in (24cm) triangles and stitch along the sides to create a square block. You now have your geese flying diagonally in your block. Make all six blocks in the same way.

7 Place your blocks in three rows of two. I chose to have my geese flying south, but you can vary the placement if you prefer. Sew the pairs into rows, and then the rows together to make the centre panel.

8 Stitch your border pieces to the side. I used an ombre fabric which means that the colour changes from the centre of the fabric to the selvedge edges. Therefore I chose to centre my border to make the most of the effect.

9 Add your top borders and trim.

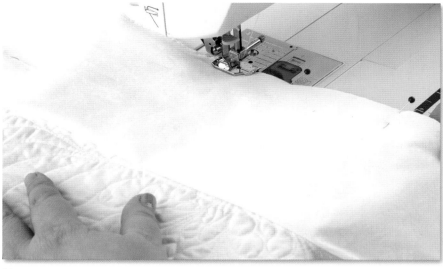

10 Layer and quilt. I chose to do some free-motion quilting in the white areas. Prior to stitching, I stabilized the quilt by stitching in the ditch with my walking foot around the flying geese blocks and along the edge of the border. This makes it much easier to keep the layers together when free-motion quilting.

DEFINITION

A basting stitch is a long stitch, so it is easy to remove.

11 I wanted to add a hanging sleeve to my project. When making a wall hanging, it is important to think about how you plan to hang your finished piece. The simplest method is to attach a hanging sleeve to the back of your project. Cut a piece of fabric measuring 9in (23cm) by the width of your quilt. Fold the short ends in ¼in (0.6cm) and press. Topstitch these ends to give a neat finish. Now place the long seams together with the fabric wrong sides together. Carefully baste the raw edges to the top edge of your quilt using a ⅛in (0.25cm) seam allowance. This will disappear inside the binding. Continue with the binding as usual.

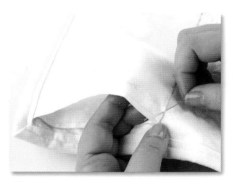

12 Once the quilt is completed, hand stitch the free edge of the sleeve onto the backing. If you do not stitch it down, the sleeve will protrude above the top edge of your quilt and be visible when you hang it.

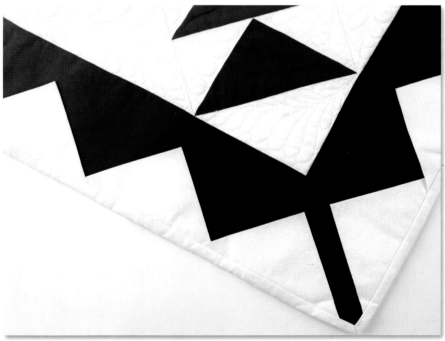

13 I thought that this quilt would look great with some prairie points in the binding, to mirror the triangles in the flying geese. Look at page 124 to see how to add these. I used six 6in (15cm) squares and basted them in opposite corners. These are quite large points and are therefore quite heavy. I have added a little hand stitch to the top of each point to stop them from pulling on the quilt when it is hung. Continue binding as normal.

QUILTED HANDBAG

This is a fabulous project to create using the flying geese block you have learnt and will be a great way to show off your new quilty skills to your friends! I am using 'Blooms' fabric by Gütermann, with Gütermann Sulky threads.

The finished size of the bag is 12 x 9½ x 4in (30.5 x 24 x 10cm).

You will need:

- 19¾in (50cm) of two outer fabrics
- 19¾in (50cm) of lining fabric
- 19¾in (50cm) of wadding
- Four bag feet, two D-rings and a magnetic clasp

Cutting instructions

We are making twelve 2½ × 5in (6.5 × 12.5cm) geese.

One geese method Cut twelve 3 × 5½in (7.5 × 14cm) rectangles from the geese fabric and twenty-four 3in (7.5cm) squares from the sky fabric.

Ruler method Cut twelve 3 × 5½in (7.5 × 14cm) rectangles from a 3in (7.5cm) strip of the geese fabric and twenty-four 3in (7.5cm) triangles from a 3in (7.5cm) strip of the sky fabric.

Four geese method Cut three 6¼in (16cm) squares from the geese fabric and twelve 3⅜in (8.5cm) squares from the sky fabric.

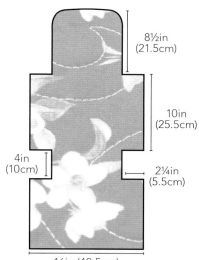

8½in (21.5cm)

10in (25.5cm)

4in (10cm)

2¼in (5.5cm)

16in (40.5cm)

Sewing instructions

1 Using your preferred method, make twelve geese blocks in total and stitch together in a row.

2 Cut two 1½ × 5½in (4 × 14cm) strips and stitch across either end of the flying geese row.

3 Cut two strips of the sky fabric 1½in (3.5cm) wide and stitch down either side of the long strip of geese.

4 Cut two strips from the geese fabric measuring 4½ × 32½in (11.5 × 82.5cm) and stitch either side of the centre block. You should now have a top measuring 16 × 32½in (40.5 × 82.5cm). You will need to trim out some of the side sections using the diagram as a guide. Use a plate as a template to curve the front flap of your bag. Repeat with the lining, so that both pieces are the same size and shape.

5 Cut the wadding ¼in (0.6cm) smaller all the way around than the bag piece outer. Using a fabric spray glue (such as 505 spray), spray onto the wadding and fix to the reverse of the bag outer. Repeat with the lining, so both pieces have wadding. You could substitute iron-on wadding which doesn't require quilting to keep it in place. I quilted along the edges of the flying geese row but you can do anything you fancy. I also used free-motion quilting for the lining.

You can see my free-motion quilting here.

WHY?

The reason we cut the wadding smaller is because it reduces the amount of fabric bulk in the seams when you stitch the bag together.

79

Adding a pocket

Cut a 6in (15cm) square of contrasting fabric. Fold the top edge over by ¼in (0.6cm) and press. Repeat the fold and topstitch to neaten. Fold the three remaining sides under by ¼in (0.6cm) and press. Pin the pocket in position and stitch round the three sides. Add a label if desired.

You can see the pocket and my label.

Making up the bag

1   Pin the sides of the bag with the right sides of the fabric together. Using your walking foot, stitch with a ¼in (0.6cm) seam allowance.

2   The cutaway section is designed to create a flat bottom to your bag so that it sits nicely when full. Fold and pin the square edge so that the bottom of the bag matches up with the side seam to create a straight line. Stitch along the edge using a ¼in (0.6cm) seam allowance to box out the bottom of the bag. Repeat for the other side. Construct the lining in the same way.

The finished shell of your bag.

Attaching the magnetic clasp

1   The magnet has two sections – one will be attached to the flap of the lining fabric inside the bag, and the other to the front of the outside fabric. Mark the magnet placements as shown in the diagram below.

2   The prongs for the magnet sit either side of the centre of the magnet so make sure you allow for that. Then use a seam ripper to carefully make two little holes for the prongs. Do not make the holes too large or the magnets will not fit securely. Flatten the prongs on the wrong side of the fabric to secure.

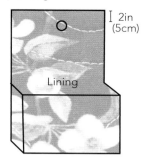
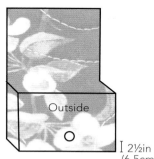

Top of bag

2in (5cm)

Lining

Outside

2½in (6.5cm)

Bottom of bag

Close-up of the magnetic clasp (back).

Close-up of the magnetic clasp (front).
This is attached to the flap of the lining inside the bag.

Close-up of the other part of the magnetic clasp.
This is attached to the front of the outside fabric.

Adding feet as a variation

Use the same method to add bag feet to the base. Place them 1½in (4cm) in from the edge of the base of the bag.

Close-up of the bag feet.

Close-up of the bag feet inserted (back).

Close-up of the bag feet (front).

Straps

1   Decide how long you want your strap to be. Cut a strip that length and 2½in (6.5cm) wide. You will also need two extra sections measuring 2½ x 2in (6.5 x 5cm) for the side straps so prepare these at the same time. Fold the strap in half and press. Cut 1in (2.5cm) strip of wadding to the same length and place inside the strap. You can use iron-on wadding or simply use a bit of spray glue to secure the wadding. Fold in the edges, including those at the short ends and press again, encasing all the raw edges. Sew down either side of the strap to secure the edges and give a neat finish.

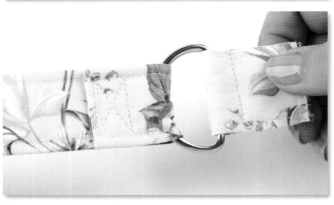

2   Fold one end of the strap over by 1in (2.5cm) and add the D-ring. Stitch the end down with a cross pattern to add extra strength. Attach the short side strap to the other side of the D-ring. Stitch across to secure the D-ring. Repeat with the other end of the strap.

3   Pin the strap to the sides of the outside of the bag and baste in place.

Constructing the bag

2 Match up the edge seams and pin it securely.

1 Make sure that the lining is inside out, and the bag is right side out. Put the outside of the bag inside the lining so that they are right sides (pattern sides) together. It is vital to ensure that the straps are tucked between the lining and the outside of the bag. If you stitch through them, the bag will not turn out correctly!

3 Sew all the way around the raw edges but leave a gap of about 5in (12.5cm) on the top of the flap for turning through – be careful as there are quite a few layers in places so take it slow. Your walking foot will be useful here.

4 This is where the gap you left in the top comes into its own! Carefully pull the whole bag the right way out through that hole. It will be tight but just be patient and go slow.

5 Once it is all out, pin the hole closed. Press the bag and then finish it with a row of topstitching all the way around the top of the bag, closing the hole as you go!

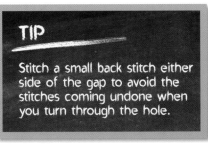

TIP

Stitch a small back stitch either side of the gap to avoid the stitches coming undone when you turn through the hole.

Sit back and enjoy your bag or, better still, start putting things in it, ready to use!

60° TRIANGLES

Equilateral triangles (as many of us learnt in school) are triangles where the sides and the angles are all equal. This means that we don't have to worry about whether we are sewing our triangles together correctly, because they always fit! Equilateral triangles are usually called 60° triangles in quilting, to differentiate them from 45° triangles or half square triangles. The fabulous thing about 60° triangles is that they can easily be used to make other shapes – two triangles make a 60° diamond, three can make a half hexagon, six will make a hexagon. This makes them a very important part of quilt design. So how do we cut them?

Method 1: Speciality ruler

This is by far the simplest way to cut triangles and there are a number of different rulers to choose from. To use a speciality ruler like these, just cut strips of fabric the height of your unfinished triangles. So, if you want triangles that finish at 3in (7.5cm), cut strips of fabric 3½in (9cm) wide (including a seam allowance).

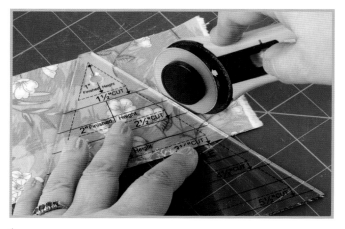

1   Line up the top of the triangle ruler with one edge of your strip and cut along each angled side of the ruler.

2   Then flip the ruler upside down and continue cutting along the strip until you have cut the number of triangles you need. Another benefit of using speciality rulers is that they have a flat notch cut out at the top of the triangle, so you can line them up for perfect piecing.

Using a template with a flat top also helps you keep your biased edges under control. Back in the basic techniques section we talked about bias stretch, and with equilateral triangles, there are two stretchy edges to manage. To keep the stretch under control, it helps to keep the straight cut edge on the edges of the row as you sew it together. If you sew the stretchy edges together as you make the row, it makes sewing the rows together so much easier because everything stretches together!

Here you can see the biased edges, which are very stretchy.

Method 2: Standard ruler

You can also use any standard quilting ruler that has a 60° angle marked on it. As with the speciality rulers, cut strips of fabric the height of your unfinished triangles. So, if you want triangles that finish at 3in (7.5cm), cut strips of fabric 3½in (9cm) wide.

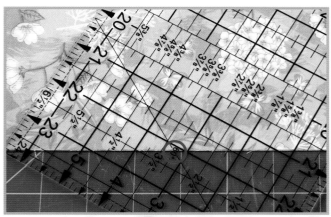

1 Align the 60° line on your quilting ruler with the bottom of the fabric strip, and cut on an angle, along the edge of the ruler. Remember to allow for the ¼in (0.6cm) seam allowance.

2 Many quilting rulers have two 60° lines: one going in each direction. If you have two 60° lines on your ruler then simply switch to the other line to cut the other edge of the triangle. Otherwise flip your ruler over and use the line to cut the third side of your triangle.

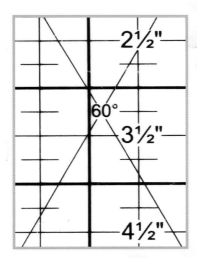

You can see the two 60° lines.

PLACEMATS

Making placemats is a great way to test out styles and techniques without using too much fabric because they are small and quick to produce. Also, there are no rules to say that all the mats need to match, so you can really have a play! This project is also a great way of using up scraps or pieces of jelly rolls that you have left over because it uses 2½in (6.5cm) wide strips. This could be a nice project to practise your hand piecing as well as your hand quilting skills.

The finished placemats measure 16½ × 12½in (42 × 32cm).

You will need:

- Eleven strips from a jelly roll (including four for binding) – I have used Liberty fabric
- 13¾in (35cm) of white fabric
- Two pieces of wadding and backing measuring approx. 20 x 15in (51 x 38cm) – you may wish to use heat resistant wadding if you think your plates might be super hot!

Cutting instructions

Use the specialty ruler method or the standard ruler method to cut your triangles for the placemats (see pages 84–85).

Diamond placemat

1 Cut a total of forty-two 2½in (6.5cm) equilateral triangles in a variety of colours. Keep two strips from the jelly roll aside for the binding.

2 Cut a total of forty-eight 2½in (6.5cm) equilateral triangles from the white fabric.

Hexagon placemat

1 Cut a total of thirty 2½in (6.5cm) equilateral triangles in a variety of colours. Keep two strips from the jelly roll aside for the binding.

2 Cut a total of sixty 2½in (6.5cm) equilateral triangles from the white fabric.

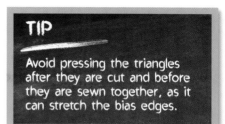

TIP

Avoid pressing the triangles after they are cut and before they are sewn together, as it can stretch the bias edges.

Here you can see the 12wt Eleganza thread by WonderFil that I used to quilt.

Sewing instructions

Using the images of the two placemats as a guide, lay out your ninety triangles.

1 Take two of the triangles and place them right sides together so that all three sides of the triangles line up.

2 Stitch with an accurate ¼in (0.6cm) seam allowance along one side (as discussed on page 84), trying to keep the straight grain edge at the top and bottom of the row. This means that you will be sewing along stretchy edges at this point so do not be too aggressive with your pieces.

3 You will find that the seam allowance hangs over the edges of the previous pair.

4 Stitch fifteen triangles together to make a row and press the seams in one direction. You will need to press each seam before sewing another triangle in place so the seams lay flat. Complete the next row and press the seams in the opposite direction to the first row. Continue until the six rows are completed.

5 The top/bottom tips of the pieced triangles in your rows should be exactly ¼in (0.6cm) from the edges of the rows if everything has worked perfectly. Match up two of your pieced rows, right sides together, with those triangle tips lined up and pin. You can check at this point that they line up – and with triangles there is often a little bit of 'wiggle room' to make them fit. Stitch the rows together, avoiding clipping the tops of the triangle points. Continue with all six rows.

6 Cut the wadding and backing slightly larger than your placemat and baste the layers together.

7 With these mats I chose to hand quilt with a contrasting thread to make it a feature. This worked well with the vintage look of the Liberty fabrics, but you can choose any method you like. This might be a good opportunity to practise your free-motion quilting with a smaller piece before embarking on a large project. Trim square.

8 Two jelly roll strips stitched together lengthwise will be enough to bind each of these placemats. Sit down and enjoy a meal using your new placemats!

CIRCLES

You are now a master of straight lines, so we are moving on to curves. These do not need to be as complicated to create as they look. Circles have impact and if you can master a curve with these simple methods then your work will take a leap to the next level.

Method 1: Appliqué method

This is a fantastic way to work with circles, because it is quick and all of the raw edges are easily tucked under before you appliqué the circle onto the background fabric. It can be used for whole circles, or the circles can be cut after they have been appliquéd down.

To avoid any unsightly raw edges, use a lightweight interface which will easily allow you to turn the edges under without any fuss.

A circular acrylic ruler (such as the EZ Quilting Circle Cut acrylic by Simplicity) makes this step easy!

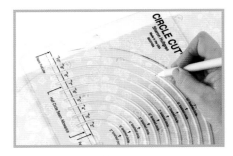

Using a circular ruler.

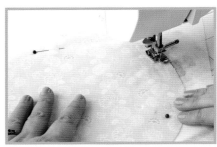

1   Cut your first circle out and lay the right side of the fabric down onto your interface.

2   Sew a ¼in (0.6cm) seam allowance all the way around the circle.

3   Trim the interface to the same size as the circle (you don't want any more fabric in the edges than you need to). Take a sharp pair of scissors and carefully snip the fabric outside of the sewn line. Snipping makes smoother curves, but take care not to snip through your stitching or your circle will come apart!

TIP

If you do cut through your stitching, simply return it to the sewing machine and go over the stitching line again.

4   Flip the circle over and cut an opening into the middle of the interfacing to remove bulk. Be careful not to cut through your fabric.

5   Turn the circle right sides out through this cut in the interfacing and smooth out the circle edges. If you have any straight sections in your circle, and you have sewn a curve, it will be caused by not snipping enough of the circular seam. Simply turn it inside out again and continue snipping until you have no straight sections.

6   Pin and stitch your circle onto an appropriate sized square (making sure that you have added ½in (1.5cm) for your block seam allowance).

TIP

If you don't have a circular ruler, hunt through your kitchen cupboards for a variety of sizes of circle – a dinner plate will work fine.

Method 2: Curved piecing

You can also introduce curves to your work with curved piecing. Curved piecing involves cutting a curve into two pieces of fabric and then stitching them together. Unlike the appliqué method, this uses less fabric and the constituent parts can be cut from strips.

The curves are created either using a template (see page 98) or with a commercial ruler.

Cutting instructions

1   Cut a strip matching the size of the background pieces. Lay your ruler or paper template on top of the fabric with the straight edges along the fabric edge. This means there is no bias stretch in the sides of your block. Cut round it. You can rotate the shape to get as much out of your fabric strip as you can.

2   Repeat with the pie template with a strip of contrasting fabric. You will need the same number of pies and backgrounds.

TIP

When I am using a paper template I stick it to my fabric using double sided sticky tape. This stops the template moving and then I can cut the curves with a pair of scissors. It is not easy to cut around paper templates with a rotary cutter because you can cut through the paper without the thickness of a ruler to guide you.

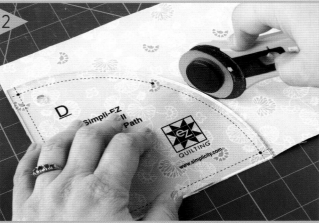

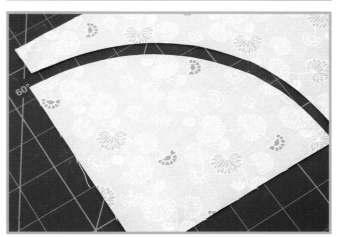

Sewing instructions

Piecing may look tricky, but persevere because it is worth it.

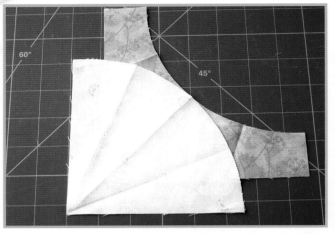

1   Pair up each background piece with a centre piece (sometimes called a pie) from a contrasting fabric. Press each piece in half to mark the centres. Then fold in half again to mark the quarter points and press.

2   You will notice that when you put your fabrics right sides together they do not match up because they curve the opposite way. This is where your pins come in handy.

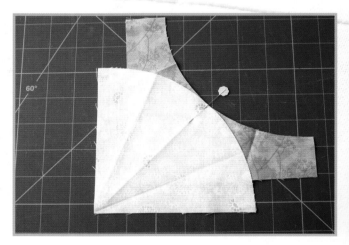

3   Place your pie and your background pieces so that the centre folds match up and pin at that point.

4   Match up the quarter points and pop a pin in each, then match up the end pieces and pin that too. Now you have five pins in your block.

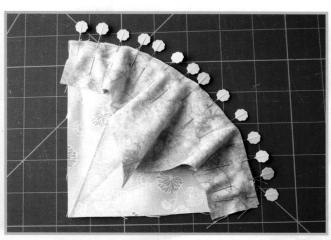

5 Use your fingers to ease the sections of fabric between the pins so that they line up, and pin in the gaps. Don't worry that your background fabric will gather.

6 You have created a fabric hedgehog!

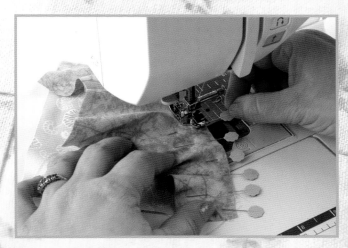

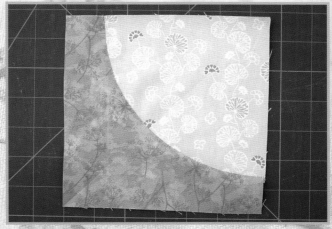

7 Using the sewing machine, keep the background piece on top, so you can see how it's easing around the curve and start stitching at one end. Remove the pins as you go.

8 Press the finished block with the fabric to the background fabric (the fabric will naturally want to go this way anyway). Make as many blocks as you need.

TIP

The key to stitching smooth curves is to take it slowly, and stop with the needle down and pivot every few stitches. Use your fingers to ease out the top fabric if it starts to fold or pucker up, but remember that the curves have a bias cut edge so be gentle to avoid stretching them out of shape.

DRUNKARD'S PATH LARGE CUSHION COVER

You will need:

- A fat quarter in pink and blue fabrics
- 39½in (1m) of plain fabric for front and backing
- Wadding to fit
- 23½in (60cm) cushion pad

'Drunkard's path' is a traditional block that can be used to create many different designs. It gets its name from the weaving movement through the quilts that mimic a path a drunk person might take. Drunkard's path is best created with a template or a ruler. The appliqué method (see page 90) can be used but it does use a lot more fabric because the back of the block is wasted, so we are going to use curved piecing with templates (see pages 91–93).

This cushion cover is quite large, but I believe that it is easier to get to grips with curved piecing on slightly larger pieces, so I have chosen 6in (15cm) finished blocks. The great thing about this block is it can be laid out in a number of ways, so you could make a set of these large cushions and have them all look slightly different.

Cutting instructions

1 Cut sixteen of the pie pieces from the plain fabric using your template or ruler.

2 Cut eight of the background pieces from the blue fabric using your template or ruler.

3 Cut eight of the background pieces from the pink fabric using your template or ruler.

Sewing instructions

1 Complete your blocks using curved piecing with templates (see method 2, pages 91–93). Trim if necessary to 6½in (16.5cm).

2 Choose your layout – for your first attempt it is probably a good idea to pick one of the designs where the circle edges do not require lining up. Place your blocks in their relative position because it is easy to get lost with so many curves.

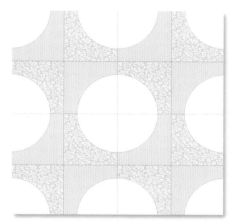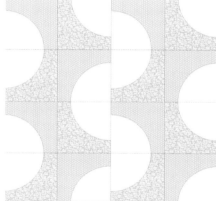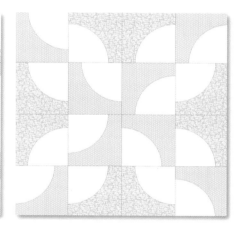

Alternative layouts for your cushion cover.

3 Take two of your blocks and place them right sides together. Sew with a ¼in (0.6cm) seam allowance, and continue sewing the whole row together. Sew all four rows together and press the seams in opposite directions. Now sew the rows together, locking the seams together as you go.

4 Layer and quilt. I decided to echo quilt through the plain fabric to focus the eye on the path. The pie shape is also a great opportunity to play with some free-motion motifs as well – just let your imagination run wild.

5 Once you have finished quilting your cushion top, trim to size and add a cushion back. You can use an envelope back (instructions on page 67) or a zipped back (instructions on pages 96–97).

6 You could of course make this into a mini quilt simply by binding it at this point.

Sewing a zip into your cushion cover

Inserting a flat zip into a cushion is simple once you know how! It will give all your cushion projects that professional look and uses less fabric than the envelope (flap) method.

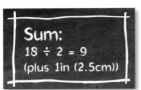

Sum:
18 ÷ 2 = 9
(plus 1in (2.5cm))

1   Measure your cushion front. You need to cut two pieces of fabric for the back of your cushion cover. Each piece needs to be the same measurement as the width of the cushion, and half the height plus 1in (2.5cm). Therefore, if your cushion front measures 18in (45.5cm) square you will need two pieces measuring 18 × 10in (45.5 × 25.5cm).

2   Place both pieces right sides together and line up the edges. On the wrong side of one of the fabric piece's edges, draw a line 1in (2.5cm) in from the edge. Now position your zip in the centre of that edge and, using dressmaker's chalk or a similar removable marker, mark where the zip starts and finishes. The zip needs to be in the centre of the cushion.

3   Remove the zip, and following your markings, sew from the edge to the beginning of the mark for the zip. Stitch a little back stitch at the end so that your stitching will not unravel later. Repeat for the other end of the zip.

4   Set your machine for the longest stitch that it will do (or select the specialist basting stitch if your machine has one) and sew the rest of the drawn line. This is where the zip will sit and the stitches are large because you will remove them once the zip has been sewn in place. You can stitch this section by hand if you prefer.

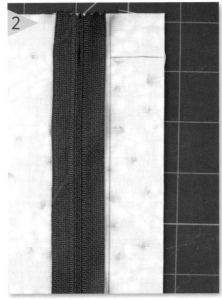

Mark 1in (2.5cm) in and the position of the end of the zip.

TIP

Use your sewing machine to do a zigzag or overcasting stitch along the long edge of each of the pieces – this will stop the fabric fraying once the zip is in place and gives a neat professional look.

5 Use your iron to press the seam open. Lay the zip face down along the basted seam making sure that the zipper teeth sit directly over the join of the seam and pin in place. With a contrasting thread, stitch a row of basting stitches down either side of the zip to secure it to the seam allowance. Make sure that the seam and zip are lined up as you sew and partly open the zip.

6 Use the zipper foot on your sewing machine to topstitch all the way around the zip. You will need to move the slider as you stitch past it which is easier when the zip has been left partly open. Make sure that you leave the needle in the fabric before you manipulate the zip, otherwise your sewing lines will be irregular.

7 Use a seam ripper to remove the basting stitches on the zip then the ones from step 4 to reach the zipper teeth below. Now you have a beautiful, professional-looking zip.

TIP

Basting the zip in place will prevent it moving as you run it through the sewing machine.

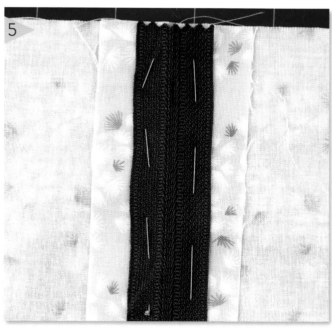

Baste the zip in place.

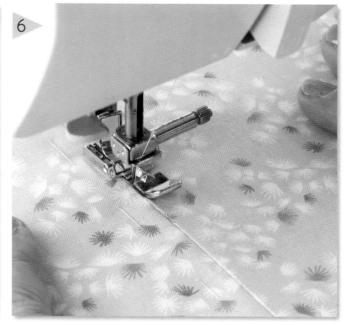

Use a zipper foot to sew around the zip.

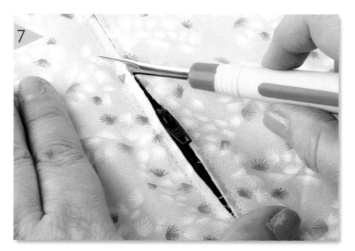

The finished zip – you are now ready to remove the basting stitches.

Templates including seam allowance

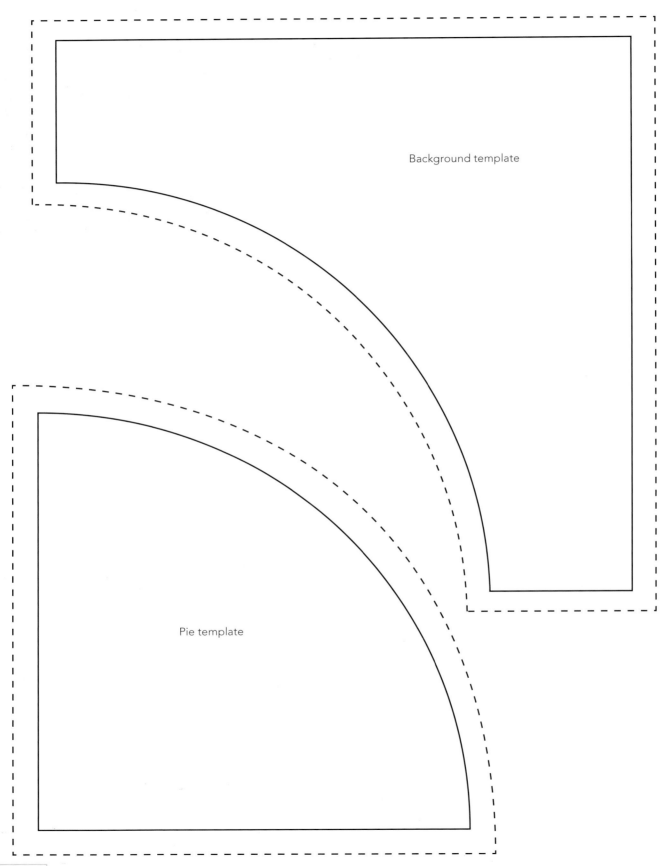

Background template

Pie template

CIRCLES QUILT

For this statement quilt, you will use the appliqué method (see page 90) to create your appliqué circles. Then you can play with the spacing until you are happy with the layout, before stitching the circles in place on top of the quilt. As the threads will show, select a colour that will not stand out too much. Also, select a complementary colour thread for the quilting design.

The finished project measures 28½ x 38½in (72.5 x 98cm).

(see page 90)

You will need:

- 19¾in (50cm) of background fabric (full width of bolt)
- Four fat quarters
- 19¾in (50cm) of border fabric
- Backing and binding fabric – you will need 29½in (75cm) for backing and 11¾in (30cm) for binding
- 19¾in (50cm) lightweight sew-in interface
- 29½in (75cm) of wadding

Making the background

1   Cut your background to measure 28½ x 18½in (72.5 x 47cm).

2   Cut three 5½in (14cm) strips to border the background. Cut one strip in half and sew to the short sides. Trim and press. Sew the remaining two strips down each of the two longer sides and press. You are now ready to start on the circles!

Creating circles

This design uses a selection of circles ranging from 10in (25.5cm) to 3in (7.5cm) wide. You can play around with your own layout by varying the size of your circles.

Here we are using the following cut measurements:

- 1 x 10in (25.5cm)
- 1 x 9in (23cm)
- 2 x 7in (18cm)
- 2 x 6in (15cm)
- 2 x 5in (12.5cm)
- 2 x 4in (10cm)
- 1 x 3in (7.5cm)

Create your circles using the appliqué method on page 90.

If you are overlapping circles, you will need to sew the back ones in place first.

Positioning your circles

1   Lay your circles out in a pleasing design, and do not be afraid to have some of them overlap into the border. Pin your circles in place to hold everything together while you sew them down.

2   Select a thread that matches your fabric choices as we don't want the stitching to stand out. Set your machine to stitch a small running stitch and test the tension and stitch size until you are happy with the result. I personally like a straight stitch. The circles require you to move the piece around a lot in order to stitch the smooth shapes, so if your machine allows it, it is helpful to set your sewing machine to sew at a lower speed than normal. Sew around one circle at a time, with your stitching as close to the edge as you can comfortably get! Sew all the circles in place.

TIP

It is a good idea to record the settings on your sewing machine, allowing you to be consistent throughout the quilt.

3 Layer your quilt. The quilting is a major part of this design and is intended to echo the circles.

4 Whichever quilting design you choose, it is a good idea to stabilize the whole quilt by stitching around the border in the ditch (which means hiding the stitching in the seams). Do this slowly and carefully as it can be tricky if you go too fast. I also like to run a line of stitching around the outside edge of the border less than ¼in (0.6cm) from the outside. This means that the border will not 'flap around' when you quilt, and the stitching will eventually be hidden inside the binding.

5 Echo the appliquéd shape. To do this, simply quilt your lines by aligning the edge of your foot a set distance away from the appliquéd circle. This means that you will be running the stitching parallel to the edges of your circle.

WHY?

The quilting is not done using a free-motion method as it is incredibly difficult to get a smooth flowing movement entirely free hand. This is where your quilting/walking foot will come in handy because it is designed to keep all the layers together when passing through the sewing machine and prevent puckering.

However, this is your quilt and you can choose to quilt it using any design that you choose. This is for your guidance only – I am not the quilt police!

6 Once you have completed one circle, you can use that as a guide for the next quilting line which now echoes the first. Two or three rows of quilting look especially attractive around the circles.

7 It is very effective to fill some of the background space with free floating circles. To do this, draw the first circle with a template and an erasable pen. Mark your circle, and use that to quilt your first line. Then use the echoing method detailed above to continue adding circles to the original. Continue the quilting into the border as this also looks great!

TIP

Always check erasable pens on fabric that you intend to mark because they may not be as effective on one fabric as on another. Also check when you haven't used your marker for a while because the active ingredient can dry up and may not disappear as well as you would like!

8 It can be fun to make the binding from a number of different fabrics to give a contemporary look – as well as making use of leftover pieces of fabric. Cut enough 2½in (6.5cm) strips from your remaining fat quarters to make a piece 12½ft (3.8m) long. Attach your binding.

BEAUTIFUL SCRAPS

You have worked your way through some of the basic shapes in patchwork and quilting. You have mastered squares, triangles, circles; you have made bags, pillowcases, quilts and placemats; and you probably have a few scraps left over. Here are a couple of fun projects that you can make in no time and will use up some of those scraps you are starting to collect…

ELEPHANT CUSHION

This cute little cushion can be as scrappy as you like and makes a great gift. The design uses 2½in (6.5cm) strips but you can make the strips narrower if that is what you have left over! Just have fun playing!

Choosing your fabrics

You can use a selection of different fabrics – including different weights and types of fabric, because the interface will prevent too much distortion. This makes it the perfect project for using scraps of fabric left over from other projects, or for making out of old clothes with sentimental attachments. My personal favourite is making the item out of men's shirts, taking advantage of the labels, buttons and cuff details. It is also fantastic made from baby clothes, jeans or giving old embroideries a new lease of life!

Marking your elephant shape

Trace the outline of your elephant template (see page 107) twice onto a large enough piece of light or medium weight sew-in interface. You can use a pencil for this because the line will be completely covered by fabric, so it will not be visible.

Cutting instructions

Cut a selection of strips measuring 1in, 1½in, 2in and 2½in (2.5cm, 4cm, 5cm and 6.5cm) wide from your fabrics.

> **TIP**
>
> Make sure that after you have drawn around your first template you flip it over before drawing the second side so that you get two different sides of the body.

> **TIP**
>
> It is a good idea to cut different measurements from the same fabric as it adds to the scrappy quality of the project.

Sewing instructions

1 Pin two strips right sides together so that the vertical seam falls mid-way between the elephant's legs. Stitch in place with a ¼in (0.6cm) seam allowance.

2 Press the two pieces of fabric flat and continue adding fabric strips in this method until the whole of the elephant is covered. Vary the width of the fabric strips as you go. Make sure that your strips are long enough to give you a good ⅝in (1.5cm) all the way around the elephant template. At this point you can use embroidery stitches to embellish your elephant, or stitch ribbon or rickrack between the strips.

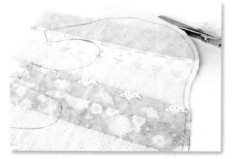

3 Once your shape has been covered, cut around your drawn line leaving a good ⅝in (1.5cm) seam allowance. This makes the elephant nice and sturdy and able to stand up to cuddles! Pin both sides of the elephant right sides together.

Tail

1 Cut two pieces of fabric out using the tail template on page 107. Sew right sides together leaving the end opposite the point open and turn through. Press.

2 Pin the tail in position between the two layers of the elephant. The position is marked on the template and will make the tail stick upwards.

3 Sew along the marked line around your elephant, making sure that you leave a space open at the back of the elephant for turning through and stuffing. A back stitch either side of the opening stops it coming undone when you stuff the elephant.

4 Trim off the corners of the feet and trunk to avoid bulk, and snip notches into all the curves so that the seams will lie smooth. Be careful not to snip through your stitch line.

5 Turn the elephant through the hole.

6 Stuff firmly, ensuring that the stuffing is pushed into the extremities to avoid unsightly bunching! Start with the trunk and then legs, and then stuff the body.

7 Sew the opening closed to complete the body.

TIP

To help you turn through the tail, use a biro.

TIP

Tease the stuffing apart before use to avoid lumps forming in your cushion.

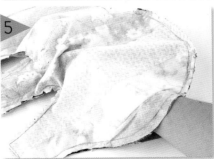

Ears

The trick to giving your elephant some real character is with the ears!
They don't lie flat to the head – they curve out!

1   Trace the ear shapes onto your interface four times (to make two sets). Sew strips onto the interface as with the body and pin the completed ears right sides together. Sew along the drawn line, leaving an opening along the straight edge for turning through.

2   Trim, leaving a ⅝in (1.5cm) seam allowance. Notch the curves as you did for the body.

3   Turn the ears out through the hole and press them flat. Slip stitch the hole closed.

4   Now to shape the ears! Mark the centre of the ear and the top quarter of the ear with pins.

5   Fold the bottom of the ear upwards at the quarter mark.

6   Then fold it at an angle at the second pin mark.

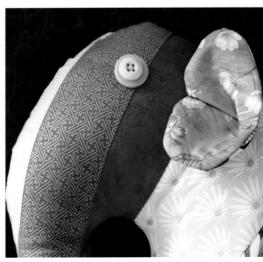

7   Pin the ears to both sides of the head, ensuring that they are level. Play around with the position of the ears and the eyes as they can really change the character of your elephant. The sharper the angle of the fold, the more the ears will stick out.

8   Sew the ears and the eyes in place with strong thread. If this is for a child, replace the buttons with felt eyes instead. Now your elephant is ready!

Finished elephant.

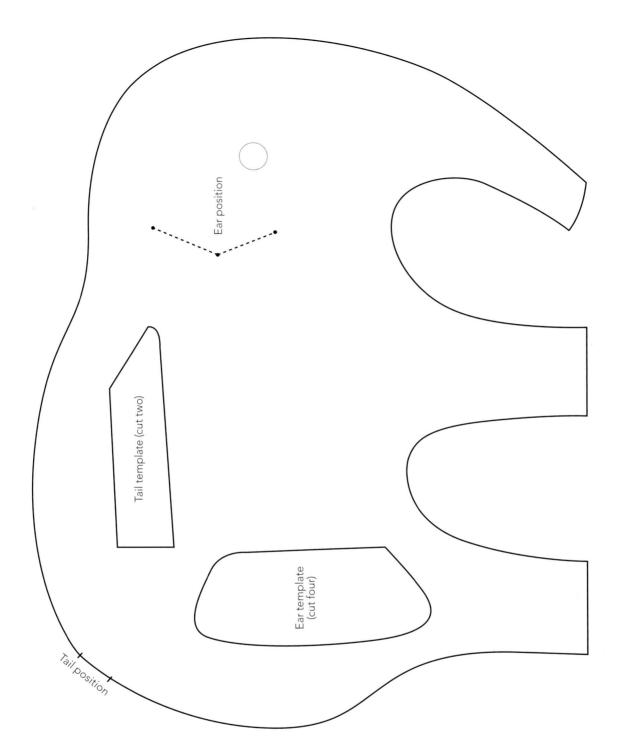

Ear position

Tail template (cut two)

Ear template
(cut four)

Tail position

This template for the elephant project has been reproduced at fifty per cent of actual size. You can, of course, make your elephant any size you like.

QUICK STRIP QUILT

This is where you can grab all of those bits of strips, binding and leftover pieces of jelly roll and put them to good use. With this design, the less the fabrics match, the better the result!

The finished size of this quilt is 36in × 36in (91.5 × 91.5cm).

You will need:

- Bits of strips – lots of them!
- 19¾in (50cm) of white for sashing
- 11¾in (30cm) of binding
- 39½in (1m) of wadding and backing

Sewing instructions

1 Start stitching pieces together until you have a piece of fabric that is at least 10in (25.5cm) wide. It is fun to vary the angle at which you sew and trim away the excess. Press all the seams in one direction.

2 Using your 6½in (16.5cm) square ruler, chop away at the fabric, creating 6½in (16.5cm) squares. It doesn't matter if you rotate the square and play around with the angles. Cut a total of twenty-five squares.

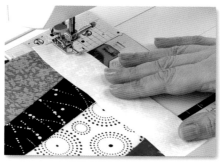

3 Cut twelve 1½in (4cm) strips from your sashing fabric. Keep four of them whole and put to one side. You will use these for the border pieces later. From the others, cut a total of twenty strips measuring 6½in (16.5cm) long. Lay out your blocks in a 5 x 5 grid, and sew one of the short strips between each block but leave the end of the row without a sashing piece. Continue until all your rows are stitched together.

4 Take one of the long strips and stitch between the first two rows. Take time to line up the blocks even though they are not directly touching. Stitch long sashing pieces between each of the rows, and use the four strips you have put aside all the way around the edge to complete the top. Then layer, quilt, bind and enjoy!

TIP

The fact that the blocks are all so different will still work because we are including sashing to unify the design. It also means that we don't need to worry about butting up all those different sized seams when we put the blocks together.

LAYERING

Layering the quilt is the process of preparing your three layers for quilting. You need to cut a piece of wadding and a piece of backing slightly larger than your quilt top. I aim for about 1½–2in (4–5cm) wider all the way around on a small to medium sized project, and a good 4in (10cm) on a double bed quilt or larger. This allows for any movement when you are quilting the layers together.

Many a lovely quilt has been thrown down in frustration when the pieces have been cut exactly, and then the layers move! So err on the side of caution and leave more than you need.

1   Cut the wadding and the backing slightly larger than your quilt.

2   Give the backing and the quilt a good iron. Layer the piece up by placing the backing wrong side up on your layering surface. Then place the wadding on next, followed by the quilt on top facing up so you have a quilt sandwich! Pin or sew the quilt sandwich together. You can make good use of quilting glue products like 505 glue to hold the layers together.

Securing the layers

To ensure that all the layers are held in place, we baste (tack) them together. Use your favourite method:

Glue

505 spray is a temporary spray designed for fabric. It is colourless and will not gum up your needle. As with all glues, spray in a well-ventilated area!

Stitching

If you don't want to use glue, you can hand baste/tack by stitching the layers together with a large stitch (about 4in (10cm) long).

Microstitching

Personally, I feel life is too short for hand basting – and I am delighted they invented the microstitch machine to save time on basting the layers! These tiny tacks can be removed with a snip once you no longer need them.

Backing

Much of the time you will find the size backing that you need for a project is larger than the size fabric you can buy from your local shop. Fabric bolt sizes are usually about 42in (106.5cm) wide (although there are some extra wide fabrics available so ask at your local retailer). If your fabric is not wide enough then you will need to sew a number of pieces together. Rather than simply stitching two bits of the same fabric together, why not make the effort to make the back look as fabulous as the front. I think it is nice to use some of the leftover fabric from the front of your quilt, or even a spare block or two to make the fabric wider. When sewing these pieces together, press the seams out flat to reduce any extra bulk.

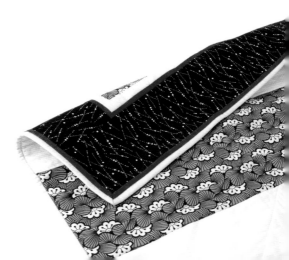

QUILTING

When you come to the end of your quilt project, you reach the toughest choice of all: how to quilt it! How you quilt can affect the overall look of your quilt, but I think it is also one of the most fun parts, because it is where you can really let loose, or keep it delicate and restrained.

First, decide whether you want to quilt by hand or by machine. Ask yourself the following questions:

What will the project be used for? Is it intended to be heavily used and washed often? If the project is expected to live a full life and be washed often, then machine quilting is the best option. Hand quilted items need to be treated with more care as hand stitching is not always as strong as machine quilting.

How much time do I have? If there is a deadline for the project, then machine quilting is definitely the way to go. Simple machine quilting can be completed in a matter of hours if you need it finished in a hurry. However, if this is a long-term project, and especially if you have hand pieced your project then it is worth taking the time to hand quilt.

How will the quilting work with my design? You need to decide if you want the quilting to be the star. If so, then hand quilting in a strong colour, or perhaps free-motion quilting (see page 117 for details) is an option. Straight line machine quilting can be used to outline areas making them appear more prominent without the quilting actually being noticeable.

What is my skill level? This should not really be a consideration. Our skill level is always zero until we try something. Quilting takes practice, so you won't get good at it until you have a go. If you are trying something new like free-motion quilting then think about using it on one of the smaller projects in this book like a cushion cover or a bag. Then, if it doesn't work out terrifically well you haven't lost anything. Also remember that you will be looking at your work with a much more critical eye than most people will, so don't be too judgemental.

Once you have chosen which method you want to use for your project, let's have a look at how you do them!

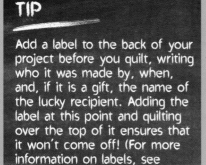

TIP

Add a label to the back of your project before you quilt, writing who it was made by, when, and, if it is a gift, the name of the lucky recipient. Adding the label at this point and quilting over the top of it ensures that it won't come off! (For more information on labels, see page 126.)

TIP

It is helpful to test your stitches by putting a little extra fabric from your quilt onto the wadding and quilting on it before you start. At least you will know what to expect once you move onto the actual quilt top.

HAND QUILTING

Hand quilting has always been a beautiful way to finish a hand pieced quilt, and it is experiencing a resurgence in popularity as many more people appreciate the art of slow stitching. In our busy world, it can be very therapeutic to take the slow lane and simply stitch.

Hand quilting can produce a softness in the work that is impossible to create any other way and it means that you do not need to invest in an expensive sewing machine to finish your hand stitched quilt.

Before we look at how to do it, let's examine the tools required:

Needles These are the most important tool for hand quilting. I personally favour the 'between' style of needle and a size 10 is ideal, as the eye isn't too big or too small, and the needle is strong enough to handle the layers of a quilt sandwich. You may wish to invest in a thimble as well. There are many different designs on the market so find one that is comfortable and works for you. Your fingers will thank you for it!

Thread This has a big impact on how your quilting looks. I prefer a thicker thread when I am quilting because I want the quilting to be the star. There are a number of speciality hand quilting threads available from different manufacturers so you have a lot of choice. Most speciality quilting threads are waxed to prevent them knotting as they go through the layers. If the thread you choose is not waxed, you can wax it yourself with a product like Thread Magic. There is no reason why you can't use stranded cotton embroidery threads if you are willing to wax.

Quilting hoops Many people like to use a quilting hoop to keep all their layers flat when quilting. There are lots of different styles available, including hand-held hoops, lap hoops and standing quilt hoops. When I am hand quilting smaller projects, I prefer not to use a hoop, but for larger projects they are a great help. When putting your project in a hoop, do not pull it too tight. The fabric will need to move up and down as you quilt, so make sure there is enough 'give' for some movement.

Now we are ready to start:

1   When hand quilting, I pay extra attention to the basting stage because the project is going to get moved around a lot as I work, so I want to make sure those layers are secure. Use whichever basting method you prefer.

2   Thread your needle with a piece of thread approximately 18in (45.5cm) long (any longer and you can get all tangled up) and tie a knot in one end. Insert your needle about 1in (2.5cm) away from where you want to start stitching, through the wadding and bring it up in the starting point for your quilt. Tug on the needle until the knot pops into the quilt top. The knot should embed itself into the wadding and will secure itself.

3   Start stitching. Hand-quilting stitches are small and keeping your stitches even is the most important part of the technique for beautiful hand quilting.

4   When quilting, keep one hand underneath the quilt so that you can be sure that your stitches are passing all the way through the layers. Use your other hand to move the needle down into the fabric and up again. Keeping lines consistent can be achieved by loading two or three stitches onto your needle before you pull the needle all the way through. Keep the tension smooth because it is very difficult to loosen or tighten your stitches later.

5   You are not working with huge lengths of thread, so you will need to change your threads often. Leave about 3in (7.5cm) of thread. Tie a knot about ½in (1.5cm) from the surface of the fabric, then pass the needle into the final hole and into the wadding (not through to the other side). Bring the needle up about 1in (2.5cm) from its starting point and tug the knot in the wadding as you did when you started the thread. I like to repeat this a couple of times to ensure that everything is firmly attached.

6   Continue quilting with a new thread.

TIP

If you wish to be accurate, six stitches per inch is a good number for beginner and intermediate quilters to aim for with their quilting.

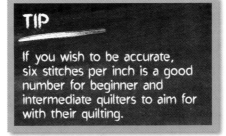

Here you can see the hand quilting used on the placemats project (see pages 86–88).

MACHINE QUILTING

You may have decided that machine quilting is perfect for your project. There are three main methods of machine quilting your layers together and we are going to explore all three:

- Method 1: Straight stitch or echo quilting
- Method 2: Stitch in the ditch
- Method 3: Free-motion quilting

Methods 1 and 2 use a walking foot. This is sometimes called a dual feed or even feed foot because that is exactly what it does – it feeds fabric through evenly. This prevents shifting and puckering that may occur with a normal presser foot, and therefore the walking foot is just as useful for garment sewing as it is for quilting. It is an all-round superstar.

The walking foot looks a little odd because it has a set of teeth to provide an extra set of feed dogs for the top of the fabric being sewn. It has an arm that attaches to the needle bar which tells the sewing machine to pull the top fabric through the sewing machine at the same rate it is pulling the bottom fabric. It is perfect for slippery fabrics, for stretchy ones, and especially for quilters who need to work with many layers. When trying to quilt through many layers, the top fabric can go one way and the bottom fabric can go another, no matter how much you have basted your layers together. The extra set of feed dogs the walking foot introduces ensures that all those layers pull through the machine at the same time, avoiding unsightly puckering!

The walking foot is perfect for straight-line quilting and the design opportunities with straight lines are limitless. Stitch in the ditch which hides your stitching in the seam and straight-line quilting are only the beginning; your walking foot can also help you stitch a variety of quilting designs with curves and even supports quilting with some of the decorative stitches on your machine. Do be aware that the foot changes the way that fabric is drawn through the machine, so some decorative stitches may not look quite as you expect them to. Always check with a spare quilt sandwich before using decorative stitches on your project.

Note that you can also stitch curves with your walking foot by changing the direction of your fabric as you feed it into the walking foot.

Walking foot. It is called a walking foot, not a running foot – keep your speed slow as you stitch.

A – Upper feed dogs

B – Machine feed dogs

Starting quilting

Whatever machine method you use, you should always bring the bobbin thread (the thread on the bottom of your machine) onto the top of your quilt. This keeps the thread out of the way while you quilt, and helps prevent a 'bird's nest' forming underneath your work and getting all tangled. It also helps if you are planning to sew your ends inside the quilt because you only need to thread your hand sewing needle once.

Position your quilt where you want to start and hold on to the top thread with your left hand. Drop the needle into the fabric and then bring the needle up again. It should pull the bobbin thread up through your fabric. Tuck it out of the way and start the quilty fun!

Finishing

There are a number of ways of finishing your machine quilting. Here are two of the most commonly used:

Back stitch I use this method if I know that the project will get heavy use and it is not going to be too obvious. At the beginning and end of each quilt line reduce the size of your stitch down to just above zero. Stitch forward a couple of stitches, and then back again before setting the stitch length back to normal and carrying on. This is especially effective if the quilting line starts in a seam line.

Burying the thread If this is an heirloom project, or a competition piece, you may wish to 'bury' your threads inside the quilt. This is the same method you use for starting and finishing threads on hand-quilted projects. To do this, make sure that you have at least 3in (7.5cm) of thread left at the end. Thread the ends into a hand sewing needle and pass the threads to the backing of the quilt. Tie a knot about ½in (1.5cm) up the thread from the fabric. Pass the needle back into the quilt near the point where the thread came up, but travel along inside the quilt a couple of inches (do not let the needle pass through onto the top of the quilt). Pull the thread tight and give it a little tug. The knot should pass through the backing of the quilt and become buried inside the wadding layer. Repeat the process if you wish.

Here is an inspirational quilt that uses free-motion quilting.

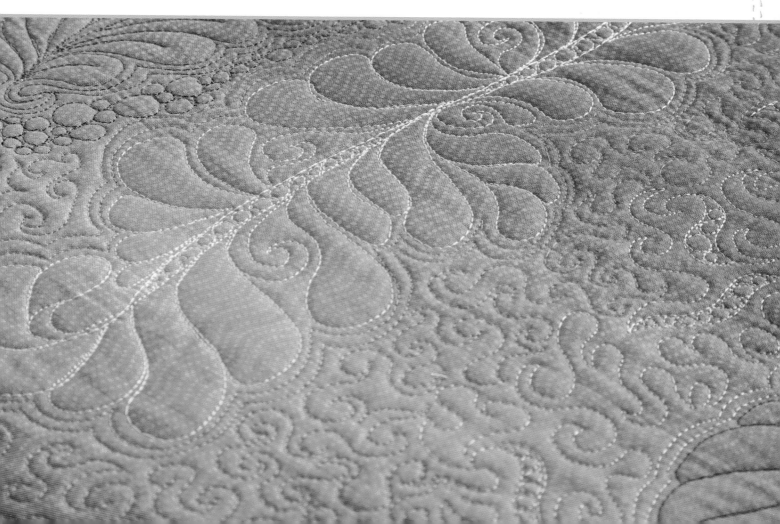

Method 1: Straight stitch or echo quilting

This is a relatively easy introduction to quilting. Using the walking foot to keep all the layers together will help get a smooth result. Echo quilting is anything that follows a line of some sort. I have used echo quilting for the shopping bag project and the disappearing nine-patch quilt – where I echoed the seams with a ¼in (0.6cm) seam allowance. I also used it for the circles quilt where I echoed the appliqué circles, and the drunkard's path cushion where the quilting adds definition to the plain fabrics. It can also be used more densely to attached appliqué pieces as shown below on the musical note.

Use the edge of the walking foot to create parallel quilting lines – great for attaching tricky appliqué shapes.

Method 2: Stitch in the ditch

The ditch is a seam line created when you sew two blocks together. This deceptively simple form of quilting is actually one of the trickiest because you have to be so accurate to hide your stitches in the ditch. If you have a wobble, it shows. However, there are definite benefits with using this design. The quilting is subtle, so it won't compete with your overall design. This is a great thing for new quilters who are not sure what design to start with. It can also cleverly enhance a particular area of a quilt by outlining it. I chose to stitch in the ditch on the flying geese bag, on the table runner and the bed runner, because I wanted the busy fabrics to be the star in all of these projects.

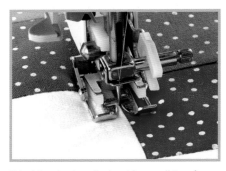

Stitching in the ditch with a walking foot.

Making it easier

- Make sure your quilt is well pressed before you start. If you have pressed your seams to one side, the ditch will become more pronounced, making it easy to follow. It is not so easy to stitch along if your seam allowance suddenly changes direction as you stitch along it. So make sure your pressing is consistent.
- You should use a thread colour that blends with your quilt top, making mishaps less obvious.
- You already have the seam lines marked on the quilt top, so you don't need to mark any new ones. Follow them carefully.
- Take it slowly. If you start to wobble you can correct it before it gets out of control.

Method 3: Free-motion quilting

Once you have grown tired of stitch in the ditch, and straight-line quilting, grab a bit of fabric and let your quilting diva loose! Free-motion quilting is the way to create truly unique designs to complement your finished quilt and make it stand out from the crowd.

Free-motion quilting can be used to add texture to the quilt – the closer the design is quilted, the stiffer the quilt will become. This means that tight quilting can be used to add structure to bags, and larger quilting will result in a snuggly, comforting quilt.

Free-motion quilting is beautiful for fancy quilting patterns, with decorative possibilities limited only by your imagination. The basic premise is that if you can draw a design on a piece of paper without lifting your pencil off the surface – then you can use it as a free-motion design.

Free-motion machine quilting requires some practice to master, but there are three main tips for getting a great result:

* Prepare
* Practice
* Relax!

Preparing your machine

For free-motion quilting, you need a special foot called a free-motion or darning foot. This type of foot has a rounded toe that travels just above the surface of the fabric. The most suitable ones have an open toe so that you can clearly see what you are doing. If you have a plastic one with a closed toe, you can cut out a section at the front with some snippers.

Next, you need to deal with those pesky feed dogs which will try to pull your fabric through your machine in a straight line – which you don't want! There are two ways you can do this:

1 Drop your feed dogs according to the instructions in your manual. If you can't do this, your machine may have a cover plate which will slide over and prevent them engaging with your fabric. If you find that you get tension issues with the feed dogs down, then you could try the second option.
2 Leave your feed dogs up, but set your stitch length to 0. This stops the feed dogs dragging your fabric in a direction you don't want to go, and can help with those obstinate tension issues.

It really helps to stabilize your quilt before you start. Free-motion is not compatible with the walking foot, so your layers can move once you get started, leading to unsightly puckering. To avoid this, use your walking foot and stitch in the ditch as much as you can, so that once you start free-motion quilting, everything will stay happily where it should! Try using this method to stabilize around a block or inside borders.

Free-motion foot.

Free-motioning feathers onto the flying geese quilt.

Suggested designs

It is useful to practise a quilt design on paper before stitching. This helps you focus your mind on how it should look and get you used to how the design will work.

Stippling (sometimes called Vermicelli stitch) This wibbly wobbly stitch can travel all over the place; the only rule is that the quilting lines must not cross. Therefore, you will need to plan a route to ensure that you do not quilt yourself into a corner!

This is a great basic stitch for covering an area and mastering it means that you have a good basis for many more quilting designs.

If you quilt far apart – 1½in (4cm) wide – you can get a very soft feeling result. If you quilt much closer together (sometimes called micro stippling) you will get a firmer result – perhaps more suitable for a bag or a wall hanging.

Stippling with motifs Stippling up to the edge of the motif gives it a raised appearance.

Draw a heart with the pen and micro stipple up to the drawn line. Iron away the pen to show your heart motif.

Developing stippling Stippling is a great starting point for other patterns. Get your notebook out and practise some other developments. For example, instead of a curved end, you can create a pointed end. At the end of a stipple, add a flower, a heart or a leaf!

Take a sandwich and play with some of these designs.

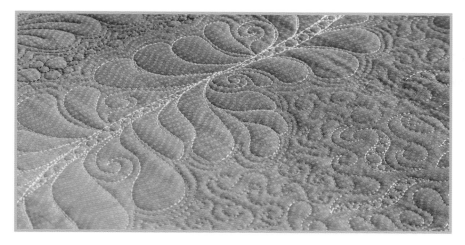

Feathers Feathers are a great feature pattern and are very versatile. They can be regular, or more flexible with uneven sides. The centres can curve, or be filled (for example – with a pebble stitch) and the edges can be echoed. It is useful to draw the centre spine but it is not necessary to draw out the whole pattern.

The feathers should flow along the spine, but there are no rules about which direction you should work in – just quilt in whatever way makes you feel comfortable.

Feathers look stunning in a feature border or as multiples on a whole cloth. Wherever you use them, you can be sure they will stand out!

Free-motion quilting with rulers

If pure free-motion feels a little too uncontrolled for you, there are now rulers to help you create a plethora of free-motion style designs. These rulers give you a line to follow, and keep your designs under control, even for beginners.

These require a special foot to stop the ruler slipping under your presser foot and a special mat that sits on top of your sewing surface to keep your fabric moving easily as you move your quilt around. There are several brands of mat available – my personal choice is SewSlip. I use my mat for all types of free-motion quilting, even when not using a ruler.

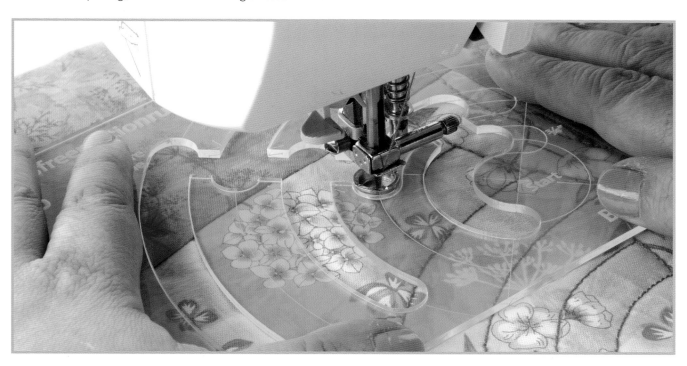

BINDING

You have made your beautiful quilt, worked hard to create a stunning quilt design, and now you are ready to bind it. Binding is the finishing edge of your quilt. It encases all the raw edges and creates a nice border.

The toughest thing to decide is what kind of binding you want to use. There are a few different options beyond the traditional binding. However, the first thing you need to do is work out how many binding strips you need to cut.

Measure all four sides of the finished project and add 12in (30.5cm) to the measurement to cover seams, corners and finishing. Divide this measurement by 40in (101.5cm) (the width of a fabric bolt) to determine the number of strips you'll need. Cut that number of strips. Most binding techniques require the strips to be cut 2½in (6.5cm) wide, unless you are making a bordered binding as on page 123.

Trim the quilt edges to the finished size to make sure the corners are square.

TIP

Always attach binding with a walking foot as it ensures that all the layers feed through evenly.

TIP

If you find that the layers of your quilt start drifting, as happens more frequently with larger quilts, extend the length of your stitch (basting stitch) and stitch ⅛in (0.25cm) all the way round. This will disappear into the seam allowance of the binding.

Traditional binding

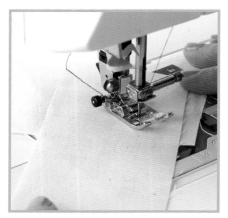

1   Place your strips together at right angles, with the fabric sides together. Sew the ends of your strips together on the diagonal.

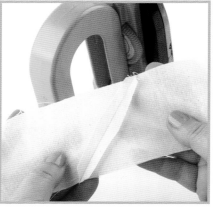

2   Trim and then press the seams open to reduce bulk.

3   Fold the long strip in half lengthways with wrong sides together and press.

4   Working from the front of the quilt and halfway along one side, match the raw edges of the binding to the edges of the quilt and then sew in place.

5   To create a neat mitred corner, sew to within ¼in (0.6cm) of the corner.

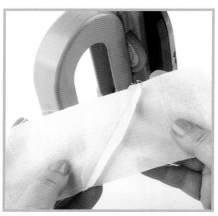

6   Then sew off the edge at 45°.

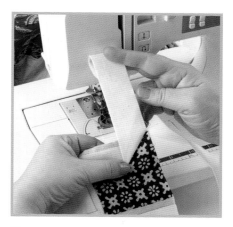

7 Fold the free end of the binding up at a 90° angle so the raw edge of the binding angles away from the quilt.

8 Fold the strip back down on top of itself, so the raw edges line up with the raw edges of the quilt. The fold you have just created will line up with the top edge of the quilt, and create a fold of fabric.

9 Continue sewing down the side of the quilt and repeat for each corner.

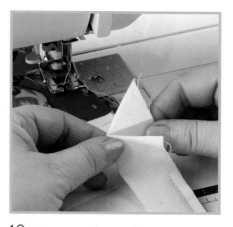

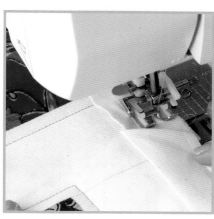

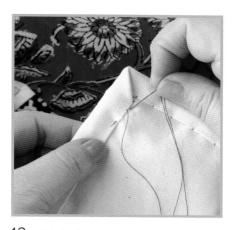

10 Before completing, fold over the raw edge of the beginning of the binding, and slot the end of the binding inside to neaten and sew in place.

11 Now sew the tail inside the fold.

12 Fold the binding over to the back of the quilt and slip stitch in place by hand. Start stitching at the place where your binding ends meet. I have used a black thread so you can see my stitches, but you would use a thread that matches your fabric. Check that your stitches aren't visible from the front. Keep your individual stitches as small as possible. You can stitch ¼in (0.6cm) apart.

Here you can see the finished binding.

Traditional binding is often the common choice, but there are more options than just the simple one.

Machine-finished traditional binding

This is often my binding of choice, because it is much quicker than hand-finished binding, and I feel that it is more resilient for items that require frequent washing like baby quilts.

   Calculate your binding, but for this method I like slightly wider binding than the traditional 2½in (6.5cm) strips, so I cut them at 2¾in (7cm). This gives me a bit more to play with once we stitch the back in place. Attach the binding using the traditional method, but do not slip stitch the back. This time we will fold the binding onto the back and clip it in place, but stitch in the ditch from the front of the binding! If you do miss catching any of the binding on the back, then a few hand stitches will usually fix that!

The front of the machine-finished binding, stitched in the ditch.

The back of the binding once it has been stitched by machine from the front.

Bordered binding

For this you have a two-colour binding. From one colour, cut strips measuring 1¼in (3cm) wide and, from the other colour, cut strips 1¾in (4.5cm) wide. In this example I have used the red for the wider strip and this becomes the inner border.

1 Sew the strips together with a ¼in (0.6cm) each seam allowance and press the raw edges together. This is where the overlap of the red is created.

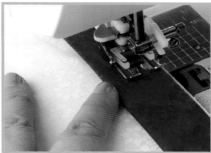

2 Begin by stitching the binding onto the back of the quilt, with the narrower strip (in this case the white fabric) on the inside and the red facing up.

3 Stitch all the way round as you would with traditional binding. Then fold the binding onto the front of the quilt and stitch in the ditch between the two colours. I am using white thread so it disappears into the white border.

Flange binding

If you like the look of the bordered binding but find the corners a little bulky, then try a flange border. This involves adding a flange or fabric strip to the binding. Cut 1in (2.5cm) wide strips of the flange material and press in half. Pin to the edges of your prepared quilt and baste along the raw edges to hold in place.

Attach the binding over the top of the basted flange using the traditional method and then fold to the back.

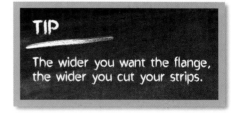

TIP

The wider you want the flange, the wider you cut your strips.

1 Pin and baste the fabric strips in place. I am using black thread so you can see my stitches.

2 Add your binding as normal, then stitch in the ditch between the flange and the binding in a matching colour.

Prairie points border

This finishing method was inspired by a trip to Nepal where the quilts are often finished with prairie points. This method gives the same effect as those traditional quilts, but is done by machine.

1   Prepare your prairie points. Cut a square of fabric and fold in half on the diagonal and then in half again to form a triangle and press. The larger the starting square, the larger the resulting point.

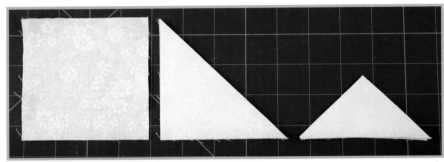

2   Working along one side of your completed quilt at a time, align the raw edge of the quilt with the raw edge of the prairie points. Adjust the points into position to create even spacing and pin into place. Baste the edges in place.

3   Apply the binding as usual, making sure all the prairie points are held in place. Larger prairie points may need a stitch in the top of the point to stop them flopping forward. This can be done with a simple hand stitch.

These are just a few different ways of presenting your binding, and adding something different to your finished quilts.

LABELLING AND CARING FOR YOUR QUILTS

Have you considered that with care, your quilts could last for decades, even centuries? These scraps of fabric that you have laboured over, and possibly handed onto family members as heirlooms, should be cherished and thought of as the works of art they are.

I have treasured quilts in my personal collection that are over 100 years old, but I know nothing about the stitcher who made them, because they didn't think to label their quilts. An artist would sign their paintings, so make sure you sign your quilts.

What to put on the label is personal preference, and it depends who the quilt is for, and whether it marks a special occasion. First, put a name and a date on the label. Feel free to state that the gift is from 'Nana Maureen', for example, but put your full name on it somewhere as well. Who knows, your quilt may end up in a museum one day and someone will want to know about you – the artist who made it.

The label itself can be as fancy or as simple as you like. With printable fabrics, embroidery machines and electronic die cutting machines, the opportunities for creativity are endless. I wrote a label in fabric pen on the back of a quilt I made my dad in 2009. It has been hugged, slept under and washed a ton of times, but the message remains. That's what the label is supposed to do!

We don't know who made this quilt, but we do know that it is 100 years old and is originally from America.

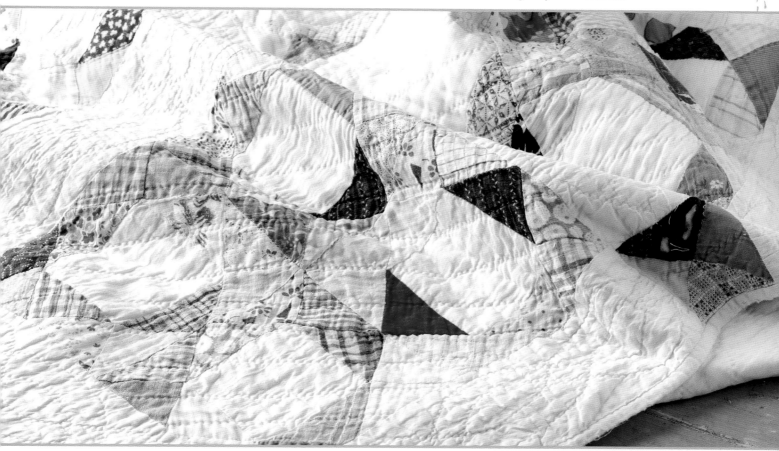

Attaching the label

If you can, attach the label to the backing prior to quilting. This way, the quilting will add extra security and hold the label in place. Appliqué your label by hand or machine – with a plain or a decorative stitch, or embed it into the binding.

Here you can see the label I have made on the back of the quilt.

Caring for your quilt

Looking after a quilt will extend its lifetime. After you have put all that work into your quilt, you don't want to see it fall apart. Take a good look at your quilt for any loose threads or damage. It is a lot easier to repair a quilt before it has been washed.

Washing your quilt

Machine washing is fine, as long as you use a cool cycle and wash with a gentle detergent. You can use colour catchers in your washing machine that will literally catch the dyes if they bleed out of any fabrics.

Hand washing is definitely recommended for vintage quilts, or handmade quilts that are more fragile. Wash in a bath filled with cool water and gentle detergent. Agitate the quilt gently for about ten minutes, then drain the soapy water, and refill with fresh water. Continue rinsing and refilling the bath until the water is clear of suds. To be extra safe, you can add a few tablespoons of distilled white vinegar to the water. This clears the quilt of any residue from the detergent, leaving it soft and bright! Repeat the rinsing process until the water is vinegar-free.

Drying your quilt

You can tumble dry your quilt – but set it to the lowest heat you can. Heat is bad for quilts – it can cause your fabric to shrink, causing unsightly puckering! I choose to tumble dry the worst of the moisture out, and then air dry it while it is still damp. Do not let any vintage or handmade quilts anywhere near your tumble dryer, even on cold! Air dry (flat if possible).

AFTERWORD

I hope that you have enjoyed your visit to my quilt school and that, as you work through the various projects, you learn new skills to take with you as you continue your journey. The idea of this book is to support you as you start, and to encourage you to continue exploring the wonderful world of patchwork and quilting. Look at the projects in this book and consider making them multiple times. Make the drunkard's path cushion into a quilt, the turned nine patch in many different sizes, and play with your quilting every chance you get.

Do not judge your work too harshly – each project is a signpost showing your improvement. You will always be your worst critic, but remember that you are doing it for the sheer joy of creating. This really is a fantastic journey that you are embarking on, and I know – I'm still taking the trip!

I would like to thank the following suppliers for providing me with the tools and materials needed for this book:

Plush Addict (www.plushaddict.co.uk); Sew, Knit, Craft (www.sewknitcraft.co.uk); Fabritastic (www.fabritastic.co.uk); Bee Crafty (www.beeingcrafty.co.uk); Create and Craft TV (www.createandcraft.com); Simplicity Rulers & Templates; Parrs Free Motion Rulers (www.parrsfreemotionrulers.com); Brother (https://sewingcraft.brother.eu/en); Gütermann's 'Blooms' fabric (https://consumer.guetermann.com/en); Janet Clare's 'Freya & Friends' fabric by Moda (www.janetclare.co.uk); Stuart Hillard's 'Kimono' fabric by Craft Cotton Company; WonderFil Speciality Threads (www.wonderfil.co.uk) and Gütermann Threads (www.guetermann.com/en)

INDEX